W9-BRD-942

Christmas with Martha Stewart Living

HOLIDAY CELEBRATIONS

RECIPES * CRAFTS * DECORATIONS

Christmas with Martha Stewart Living

HOLIDAY CELEBRATIONS

RECIPES * CRAFTS * DECORATIONS

Copyright © 2004 by Martha Stewart Living Omnimedia, Inc., 11 West 42nd Street, New York, New York 10036; www.marthastewart.com. All rights reserved. No part of this book may be reproduced or transmitted in any form or by any means, electronic or mechanical, including photocopying, recording, or by any information storage and retrieval system, without permission in writing from the publisher. *Originally published in book form by Martha Stewart Living Omnimedia, Inc., in 2004. Published simultaneously by Oxmoor House, Inc. and Leisure Arts. A portion of this work was previously published in MARTHA STEWART LIVING.* *All projects described in this publication are for private, noncommercial use only. No rights for commercial use or exploitation are given or implied.* *Printed in the United States of America. ISBN 0-8487-2845-9 (hardcover) 0-8487-2846-7 (paperback)*

CONTENTS

INTRODUCTION

C*onsider the holiday parties you have* known and loved: Christmas Eve dinners with just your immediate family, around a table polished by the memories of generations; neighborhood open houses lasting all day, where everyone is comfortable enough to come and go and even come back again; sparkling New Year's Eve gatherings; casual afternoon lunches with groups of friends settled into easy chairs. It seems that most everyone loves a party, but not everybody throws one in quite the same way—especially during the holiday season, when all the invitations (mixed in with Christmas cards, of course) can make the mailbox bulge to overflowing.

Planning your own holiday party can be a merry event in itself. This year we at *Martha Stewart Living* share some of our favorite seasonal entertaining ideas, where theme, food, décor, location, and crafts come together to create different moods to match a variety of desires for company and formality. Take it all in, and feel free to mix and match menus, decorations, and party favors as you choose. All we ask is that you make celebration the means *and* the end. Happy holidays from all of us.

CANDY-SHOP PARTY FAVORS
Opposite: Create a candy-counter-style display with candy jars for guests to take home. Collect used jars (or buy inexpensive containers), and fill them with a selection of candies, arranged in patterns or simply layered. Embellish lids with decorative papers or paint, and trim with ribbon and gift tags. Below: For a sweet and colorful centerpiece, stack cake stands, then top them with vases or drinking glasses full of candy canes and lollipops. Fill in display with wrapped peppermint candies.

Joy!

good things

Decorative details and clever entertaining ideas count more during the holiday season than at any other time of year. Even the smallest touch can have a big impact on any party. Here are more than a dozen timely ideas for the table, bar, mantel, and more. Spread the seasonal joy in such little ways and your guests' pleasure will surely bring it right back to you.

MY GLASS, YOUR GLASS

With tags made from quilling paper (available at crafts stores), guests can identify their drinks at a glance. Curl thin strips tightly around a cocktail skewer, leaving an inch or two straight at one end. Set out coils and a white-gel pen near your glassware; each guest can label her tag, then curl it around the stem of her glass.

SPARKLING BUBBLY

For a cheery way to present Champagne, rub the rims of fluted glasses with lemon wedges, then dip them in shimmering colored sanding sugar (available at baking-supply stores). Let sugar dry at least thirty minutes before filling glasses.

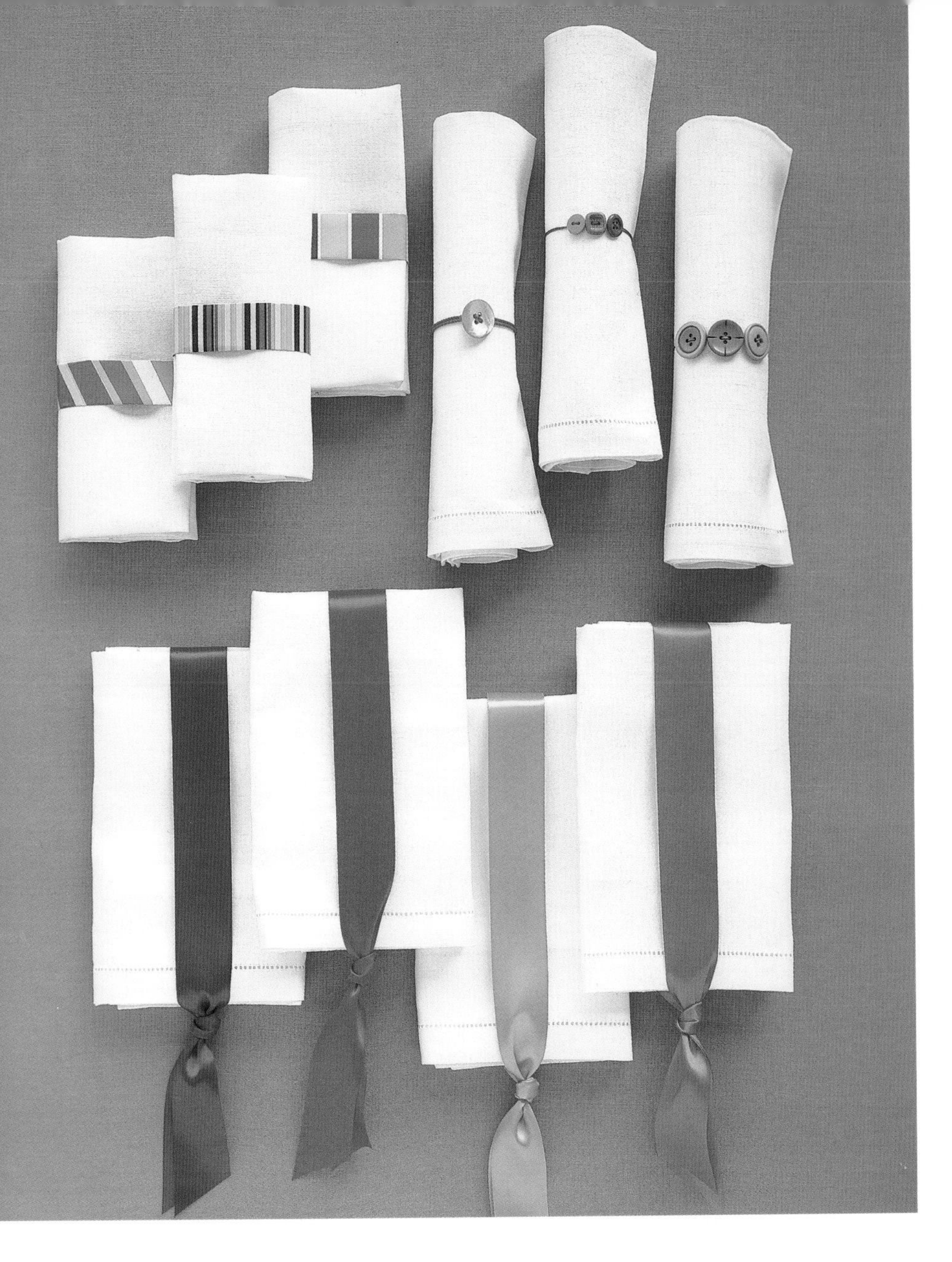

PLACE-CARD "CANDIES"

What could be sweeter? Cut out 3-inch ovals from colorful card stock. Punch a hole at ends of ovals, and then neatly write guests' names with black ink. Thread ribbon scraps, each about 6 inches long and 1½ inches wide, through holes and behind backs of cards. Notch the ribbon ends. Set a labeled card at each table setting.

MERRY NAPKINS

Dress up a bunch of ho-hum white napkins with napkin holders made from materials you probably already have at home.

PATTERNED SCRAPS Use bright lengths of leftover wrapping paper to give napkins flair (top left). Fold the edges of the wrapping paper so holders have a clean, hemmed look; then wrap them around folded napkins. Use double-sided tape to join the ends of the paper on the underside of the napkins.

BUTTONS A few mismatched buttons and bits of vibrant cord give white napkins a playful splash of color (top right). Thread thin cord, string, or embroidery floss through buttonholes. Roll napkin, wrap cord around it, then tie on the napkin's underside. Varying the colors and numbers of buttons used adds a bit of whimsy.

BRIGHT RIBBONS Tie up plain, folded napkins in bursts of red, pink, or any other bright color (bottom). Wrap several inches of remnant ribbon—try satin, grosgrain, or taffeta—lengthwise around each of your napkins, knotting the ribbon at the bottom and pulling it taut. Snip ends at an angle.

RIBBON TREES

These tiny trees don't need trimming—they *are* trimming. All that's required to make them is wide, flat green ribbon, a sewing needle and thread, and a hot-glue gun.

1. Use ribbon to make graduated tiers. Accordion-fold a length of ribbon 15 times for 8 points.(The distance between the folds will determine the tree's breadth; if using ¾-inch-wide ribbon, try 2½-inch folds for the bottom tier.) Pressing folds together, pull a threaded needle through the open ends and folds that will become the center of the tier, leaving 8 folds on outside of ribbon. Loop, knot, and trim thread, and fan out folds. Make at least 5 tiers, decreasing distance between folds by about ½ inch each time.

2. To assemble, dab hot glue onto center of each tier, stacking from largest to smallest.

MIX-IT-YOURSELF HOUSE COCKTAIL

Let a guest be his own bartender with this clever arrangement. Select a favorite mixed-drink recipe; then print it out, and display it on a bar or small table. Set out the necessary ingredients, and watch as your friends shake things up. Here's the recipe for our Happy Holidays Cocktail: Pour ½ ounce each of vodka and Cointreau into a glass with ice. Add 2 ounces cranberry juice and 3 ounces Champagne. Top with cranberries and a vodka-soaked orange slice.

GLASS GARDEN

You don't need flowers in winter to make a colorful display: Place glass ornaments under a garden cloche (a bell-shaped glass cover that functions as a miniature greenhouse for outdoor plants). Filled with sparkly tree trimmings, they add radiance to the tabletop. To fill, turn a cloche upside down and balance it inside a cup (above). Place ornaments inside, then invert a plate over the open end. Carefully turn cloche and plate right side up.

Molly

TWIG PLACE-CARD HOLDERS

TOOLS AND MATERIALS

Evergreen branches (about the thickness of a pencil); floral shears; hot-glue gun; card stock; calligraphy or felt-tip pen; small evergreen sprigs

With floral shears, cut slim evergreen branches into 4-inch segments. Trim off any nubs. Holding two segments of about the same thickness, adjust them to fit together snugly—this might require some twisting, turning, and further trimming. Turn pair of branches over; run a line of hot glue across the pair's width, ¼ inch from each end. Press branches together, and let glue dry. Write a guest's name on a 1-by-2½-inch piece of card stock. Slip the place card between the branches, and then tuck a small evergreen sprig into one end.

GLITTERY DEER DECORATIONS

TOOLS AND MATERIALS

Toy deer; paintbrush; white glue; glitter

1. Holding a toy deer by one leg, use a paintbrush to coat head, body, and other three legs with a thin, even layer of white glue.

2. Spoon glitter onto deer; gently shake excess into bowl. Let dry. Repeat process on last leg, then touch up any bare spots by dabbing them with glue and spooning on more glitter.

CINNAMON CANDLES

TOOLS AND MATERIALS

Pillar candles at least 3 inches in diameter; 8- and 16-inch cinnamon sticks; floral shears; hot-glue gun; small dishes or coasters

Cut cinnamon sticks to height of candles with floral shears. You'll need about 20 lengths for a 3-inch-wide candle. Run hot glue along length of stick; affix it to side of a candle. (Use low-temperature setting of gun to minimize melting.) Once dry, glue another stick snugly against it; repeat to cover candles (right). Put finished candles on dishes.

A BETTER WAY TO HANG WREATHS

By suspending your holiday wreath from the top of the door rather than the center, you can avoid making holes in the more visible areas of your woodwork.

1. Cut a piece of 3-inch-wide satin ribbon that's long enough when doubled to hang wreath at desired height. Loop ribbon around back of wreath form. Join ribbon ends, and fold them over by ½ inch.

2. Secure ribbon to top of door with a few thumbtacks.

NATURAL LIGHT

Candles set in a pool of cranberries create a simple, seasonal centerpiece. Dribble a little melted wax from each candle into white serving bowls to anchor candles. Set candles in place, then partially fill bowls with water; float fresh cranberries on top.

EASY GARLAND INSTALLATION

TOOLS AND MATERIALS
Teacup hooks; rope; scissors; floral wire on a paddle; evergreen garland; artificial berry sprays; wide decorative ribbon

1. Attach teacup hooks to opposite sides of the top of a window frame. Arrange rope around window, making knotted loops where rope meets hooks (as shown). Cut rope at bottom of window frame, and take down from window.

2. Using floral wire, attach evergreen garland to rope; intersperse berries, wrapping onto garland with wire. Hang garland, placing loops on hooks, and tie ribbon to garland at corners.

CHAPTER one

A FAMILY GATHERS AT HOME *for the* HOLIDAYS

E*ach family has its own way of spending Christmas* together. The bigger and more widespread the group, the more challenging the preparations become. Skip and Clare Hellewell, head of a sixteen-member clan, including their six children, children-in-law, and an ever-growing number of grandchildren, get a jump on the task by leaving their home in southern California just after Thanksgiving to ready the homestead in Utah. When the family is at last together, after traveling from points east and west to Midway, a small mountain town nestled in the Rockies, the only challenge left is a happy one: finding just the right Colorado spruce to bring indoors and decorate. And though the whole family will fit snugly in the farmhouse built in the late nineteenth century by Clare's grandfather John M. Huber, getting everyone around the tree to trim it is always a sport sparking plenty of merriment itself.

LET IT SNOW *Opposite: This high valley in the Rockies' Wasatch Range in Utah is almost guaranteed snowfall at Christmastime. But flurries or more won't deter the Hellewells from the group effort of fetching a tree. Above, from left: Apple pie is one of the many sweets on offer for the holidays. Paper snowflakes made from delicate doilies adorn the Christmas tree.*

Once the tree is selected, hauled home, and dressed up for the festivities, the family heads en masse to the kitchen. Daughters Brooke (a senior art director at *Martha Stewart Kids*) and April bake the facade of a gingerbread house, designed and decorated to resemble the Hellewell home in miniature. Soon others join in the act. For five generations, the family has followed the farmer's time-honored

RED, WHITE, AND MERRY *Opposite: Beneath a wreath of tallow berries, a gingerbread house facade made by Brooke and April is flanked by candles, some set in votive holders made of scooped-out apples, reflecting ancestor Johannes's reputation as Midway's Johnny Appleseed. Mismatched dining chairs are decked with garlands of bright-red rickrack and seating-card tags. This page, from left: In keeping with the celebration of holiday and heritage, the table is decorated in red and white; dimity runners are laid crosswise, in lieu of a tablecloth, and each place setting is topped with a candy cane. For an hors d'oeuvre, everyone dips into cheese fondue, a dish with Swiss origins.*

menu CHEESE FONDUE * ENDIVE AND RADISH SALAD

SMOKED HAM *with honey-orange glaze* * VANILLA APPLESAUCE * POTATO ROSTI

GREEN BEANS *with spaetzle* * ORANGE SPIRAL ROLLS * MILE-HIGH APPLE PIE

CHOCOLATE- AND BUTTERSCOTCH-CHIP COOKIES * BRATSELIES

ALMOND SHORTBREAD COOKIES * CHOCOLATE FUDGE * PEANUT BRITTLE

ALL TOGETHER NOW *Opposite: Linens, bowls, platters, and serving pieces in red and white create a unified look on the buffet table. Candles in red and milk-glass holders are placed along the windowsills. This page, from left: The choices on the Hellewell holiday menu are many, and though only some are Swiss, all are completely irresistible, as one generous serving shows. Under the glowing Christmas candle tree, little ones get the most special places at the dinner table: their parents' laps.*

SWEET CHARITY *Clare Hellewell's mile-high apple pie makes a grand appearance every Christmas season. Chewy and crisp sweets include chocolate- and butterscotch-chip and almond shortbread cookies. Opposite: The whole family pitches in to create gift boxes, each one filled with peanut brittle, chocolate fudge, cookies, and store-bought candies. Tags stamped with the letter* H *adorn the boxes.*

H
h
h
h
H

projects MAKING AND DECORATING A GINGERBREAD HOUSE FACADE

MAKING FACADE AND SUPPORTS

TOOLS AND MATERIALS
Gingerbread Dough for Houses (see recipe, page 112); photograph or drawing of house to be copied; tracing paper; felt-tip pen or pencil; card stock; straightedge; scissors; rolling pin; Silpat or other nonstick baking mat; all-purpose flour; paring knife; utility knife

1. Using a photocopier, enlarge to desired size the photograph or drawing of the building you would like to render in gingerbread. (Make sure rendering will fit on your largest baking sheet.) Place a sheet of tracing paper over the enlarged image, and trace it with a felt-tip pen or a pencil. Be sure to trace all the exterior details and features of the house—doors, windows, eaves, shutters, shingles—so you can outline with icing later. Copy the tracing onto a sheet of card stock to make a template, and cut out.

2. Roll out gingerbread dough on Silpat baking mat as instructed in recipe. Lightly dust dough with flour so template won't stick. Place template over dough, and cut out facade of house with paring knife. Remove excess dough from around template, and set aside.

3. Cut out windows. Gather together scraps of dough, and roll out; cut out shutters for windows and supports to hold the facade up (you will need two; see template, page 29).

4. Place facade, shutters, and supports on Silpat baking mat set atop a baking sheet, and bake according to recipe directions. Once cool, place template over baked gingerbread. Using utility knife, lightly score along roof lines, shingles, and door; the lines will serve as guides to pipe icing when decorating. Gingerbread can be stored on baking sheets, covered with plastic wrap, for a few days. Decorate facade following directions on page 28.

HOLIDAY HOMESTEAD
Opposite: Brooke and her sister April's gingerbread-house facade was based on a drawing of their family homestead in Midway, shown (right) dressed with lights, greenery, and snow for Christmas. The facade stays upright on the mantel with two gingerbread supports attached to its back.

GETTING STARTED *Before you begin working, remove any jewelry that might become encrusted or inhibit your decorating. Start by attaching the proper tip—Ateco #2 for piping and Ateco #3 for flooding—to a pastry bag fitted with a coupler. Form a cuff by turning down the top three inches of the bag. Place the empty bag upright in a tall drinking glass. Spoon the icing into the bag until it is one-half to two-thirds full, and close with a twist tie or rubber band. Fill all the bags you will need. To prevent the icing from drying and clogging the tip, place a damp paper towel in the bottom of the glass, and place the bag, tip side down, in the glass. Alternatively, put a toothpick in the end of each pastry tip. Icing will keep up to two days in the bags at room temperature or for several weeks in an airtight container in the refrigerator. Always stir icing before using if it has been stored. (If you color the icing, the color may separate during storage; gently massage the bag to remix.)*

DECORATING TECHNIQUES

TOOLS AND MATERIALS
2 pastry bags with couplers and #2 and #3 tips; Royal Icing (see recipe, page 112); offset metal spatula; pastry brush or small paintbrush; 1 egg white lightly beaten with 1 tablespoon water; spoon; white nonpareils or sanding sugar

1. Using a pastry bag fitted with a #2 tip and filled with icing, outline any areas you want to cover completely, such as eaves or turrets (use scored lines as guides); let set 5 to 10 minutes. While it sets, "draw" shingles by piping along scored lines, using the same tip. Then, with an icing bag fitted with a #3 tip, draw tight zigzags within the outlined areas to fill in (this is known as flooding). While still wet, spread icing evenly with offset spatula.

2. When icing is dry, use a #2 tip to pipe decorative lines on top of flooded areas, if desired. Here, we're making roofline trim for a three-dimensional effect. Decorate shutters as desired.

3. If desired, lightly brush some uniced areas of gingerbread with egg wash, then, using a spoon, liberally sprinkle nonpareils or sanding sugar over top. (Work quickly, as egg whites dry rapidly.) Let sit 20 minutes, then remove any stray nonpareils or sugar with a pastry brush or paintbrush.

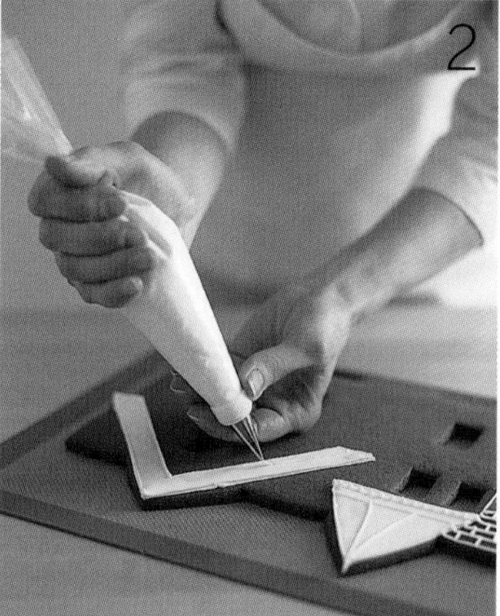

MAKING WINDOWS

TOOLS AND MATERIALS

Nontoxic molding clay; rolling pin; Silpat or other nonstick baking mat; ruler; utility knife; Sugar Syrup (see recipe, page 113); pastry bag fitted with #2 pastry tip and filled with Royal Icing

It is important to use windowpanes as soon as possible after making them; if stored, they become tacky and impossible to work with. Don't make the sugar syrup until the molds are ready.

1. Make windowpane molds: Roll out molding clay ¼ inch thick on Silpat baking mat. Measure windows of house; add ½ inch all around. With a utility knife, cut out molds from clay using these measurements. Make syrup; immediately pour it into the molds. Let set in molds until completely dry, about 1 hour. Carefully lift clay, leaving windowpanes behind. Turn house over so you can work from the back of the facade.

2. "Glue" panes into window frames: Outline back of frame with icing by piping a thick line ¼ inch from edge of frame. Press "glass" into place. Let icing dry completely, about 1 hour. Turn house right side up. Embellish windows, if desired, following instructions on page 30.

ATTACHING SHUTTERS AND SUPPORTS

To attach shutters, pipe a very thick line of icing along the edges of the windows. While still wet, attach shutters at a slight angle. If necessary, prop shutters up with a ½-inch piece of toothpick or crumpled paper towel to hold them slightly away from front of house as the icing dries. Once shutters are set, attach supports for house to either end: Pipe icing along the angled edge of support, using a #3 tip. Hold support, narrow end up, flush against one side of the house until set. Repeat on other side of the house.

GINGERBREAD HOUSE SUPPORT TEMPLATE

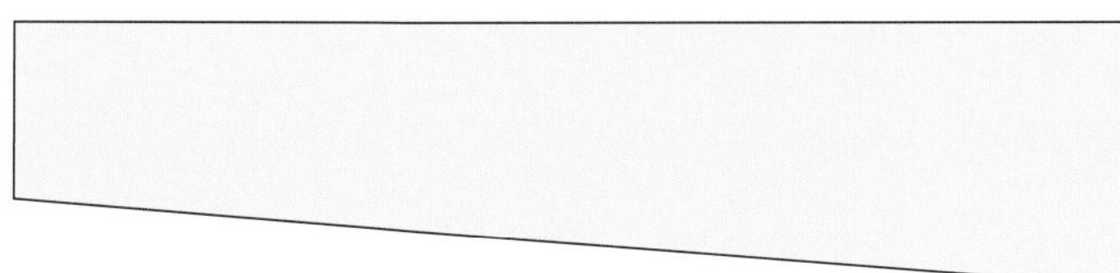

SUPPORT TEMPLATE Enlarge template on a photocopier to height of your house. Trace onto card stock, and cut out. Use template to cut out two supports from gingerbread.

HELPING HANDS *Brooke and April enlist the help of their young niece, 5-year-old Anne. With their guidance, Anne sprinkles sanding sugar over the roof of the gingerbread house so it will sparkle like sunlight reflecting off of snow.*

DECORATING DETAILS FOR GINGERBREAD

Think of gingerbread and icing as a blank canvas and paint. Here are some suggestions for materials and techniques you can use, but remember that there are no rules—let your imagination guide you.

1. SQUARE-PANED WINDOW WITH SNOW Pipe a thick, straight border of icing around window. Pipe mullions (dividers) onto pane with a #2 tip, using graph paper placed beneath pane for accuracy. Once pane is dry, pipe a thick layer of icing across bottom of window; sprinkle with sanding sugar while icing is still wet.

2. ROUND-SHINGLED ROOF Round white candy wafers applied in an overlapping pattern simulate rooftop shingles. Pipe a dab of icing onto the back of each wafer and work in rows, beginning at the bottom and working your way up, overlapping slightly as you go.

3. TRIANGULAR ROOF PATTERN Using a pastry bag fitted with a #2 tip, pipe a series of equidistant horizontal lines across roof (you should score these lines before piping, as directed on page 27). Then pipe a series of same-size triangles that connect the lines, leaving negative spaces in the dimensions of the triangles (don't worry if they are not perfect). While icing is still wet, sprinkle sanding sugar over triangles to add sparkly detail.

4. SPECKLED SURFACE Flood the surface with icing, then sprinkle with crushed candy canes while icing is still wet. This application creates a faux-stucco surface.

5. BRICK SURFACE Pillow candies are "glued" with icing into horizontal rows to simulate brick. We chose white candies, but you can use other colors if you wish. You can also use candy-coated chewing-gum squares for a similar effect.

6. ICICLES COVERED WITH SNOW Pipe a thick line of icing across the top of your surface; then pipe icing into icicle shapes below line. Sprinkle with sanding sugar while "icicles" are still wet.

7. ARCHED WINDOW Using a pastry bag fitted with a #2 tip, pipe a pair of horseshoe shapes around an arched window frame, beginning and ending at bottom of window (allow room on top of outer line for keystone). Fill in arched shape with a series of lines to connect. Pipe a pair of parallel lines below window, and connect with a series of vertical lines. Using graph paper placed beneath pane, pipe mullions (dividers) directly onto window's surface.

8. SCALLOP-PATTERNED ROOF WITH SNOW Pipe thin curved lines from top to bottom of roof. Then pipe horizontal lines of icing in a scalloped pattern, using a smaller icing tip for top lines and larger tips for bottom lines. Peaks of scallops should meet up with vertical lines. While icing is wet, sprinkle with sanding sugar to make "snow."

9. SHINGLED ROOF WITH SNOWBALLS Make a round-shingled roof (see number 2, above) using chocolate nonpareil candies. Place ball candies on top, between the nonpareils, to add another decorative element.

1. SQUARE-PANED WINDOW WITH SNOW

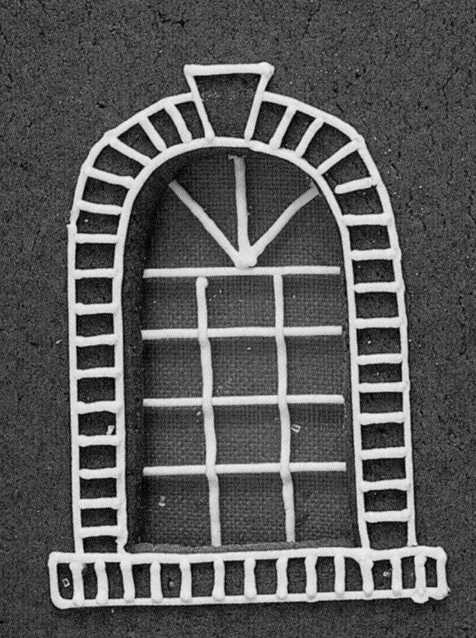

7. ARCHED WINDOW

decorating glossary

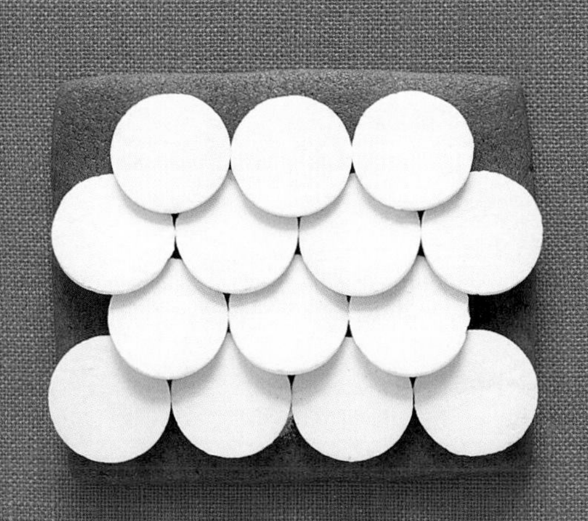

2. ROUND-SHINGLED ROOF

3. TRIANGULAR ROOF PATTERN

4. SPECKLED SURFACE

5. BRICK SURFACE

6. ICICLES COVERED WITH SNOW

8. SCALLOP-PATTERNED ROOF WITH SNOW

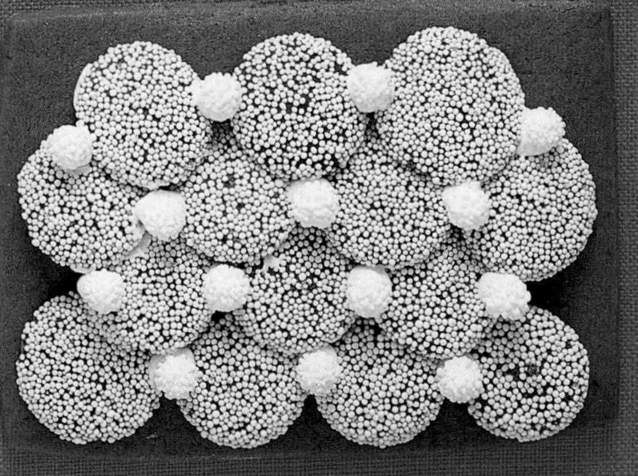

9. SHINGLED ROOF WITH SNOWBALLS

CHAPTER two

TREE-TRIMMING DESSERT PARTY

A*t no other time of the year are* spectacular desserts and sparkling decorations in greater abundance than during the winter holidays. This gave Martha a novel idea: Why not combine her passions for holiday decorating and dessert-making into one occasion? Inviting others to help trim the tree would make the task itself cause for celebration, turning the home into a festive hub of holiday activity.

For Martha, the best part of getting the house ready for the holidays lies in finding a theme—one inspired by a recent discovery, perhaps, or a childhood memory. In this case, the decorations honor Martha's heritage. Her grandparents came from Poland, where Christmas is considered a time of renewal. Ornaments made of straw symbolize thanksgiving for the harvest and hope for the new year, so for the party, handmade straw ornaments and gilded eggs are rendered in lustrous shades. Glass balls in varying sizes are wired together to resemble a bunch of grapes. Touches of gold also grace the table, in tender cornmeal cookies, caramel shards atop a layered torte, and apricots peeking through buttery tea cakes. As guests search for the choicest spot on the tree for each ornament, they look forward to their reward: a plate arrayed with inspired delectables.

GOOD AS GOLD

Opposite: Martha and her niece Kristina put the finishing touches on gifts for their guests. The table-top tree in the parlor, a small spruce, was carefully pruned and clipped, leaving five horizontal rows. Its form is reminiscent of an old-fashioned feather tree. This page: Kristina holds an ornament made by braiding strands of arrow wheat together into a wreath, then burnishing it with gold mica powder and attaching a gold bow.

ALL THAT GLITTERS

Opposite: The foundation of the lattice-topped apple-rosemary tart is a pastry dough made with ground walnuts. Honey-glazed walnuts and fresh rosemary sprigs make fitting garnishes. This page, clockwise from top left: Gold-wrapped presents come with an extra gift—a handmade ornament attached to the top—so each guest has a keepsake from the party. Glass ornaments and eucalyptus leaves fill a footed porcelain basket on the mantel; a smaller basket holds walnuts in their shells. On close inspection, the tabletop tree reveals a variety of straw ornaments—some tied with ribbon bows, others left unadorned. In Poland and Ukraine, sprigs of wheat augur a healthy crop and prosperity in the new year. The decorations have been given a burnished glow using metallic powders in a range of hues, from light copper to deep verdigris.

ROOM FOR DESSERT

Opposite: Most of the colors in the room—not just of the food, but of the serving pieces, linens, and decorative touches as well—stay within the same golden color palette, lending the setting a sense of harmony. A cluster wreath of ball ornaments hangs on the dining room door. This page, left: Coupe-style glasses of muscat wine frame a plate of rich chestnut truffles. Bottom left: Orange-flavored cornmeal dough is piped into S-shaped cookies using a pastry bag fitted with a large star tip.

menu APPLE-ROSEMARY TART * APRICOT TEA CAKES * ORANGE-CORNMEAL COOKIES * CHESTNUT TRUFFLES * POACHED PEARS *with three sauces* * DOBOS TORTE

SUGAR COATING *Opposite: Guests have their choice of embellishments for poached pears—rich chocolate sauce, a luscious whipped-cream-and-mascarpone combination, or a spicy syrup made from a reduction of the wine in which the fruit was simmered. This page, from left: On a glass plate with golden harvest symbols, an individual tea cake reveals its apricot and almond filling. Dobos torte, named for Austrian pastry chef Josef Dobos, is made with thin slices of yellow cake brushed with hazelnut simple syrup, then frosted with caramel buttercream; a coarsely chopped sheet of caramelized sugar is scattered over the top.*

GILDED EGG ORNAMENTS

TOOLS AND MATERIALS
Quail or chicken eggs; pins; skewer; small paintbrushes, one pointed; water-based sizing; mica powder in gold, green, and copper; soft artist's brush; dust mask; rubber band; off-white latex enamel paint; foil-paper trim and beads; white glue; model cement; gold cord

1. Poke a pin into each end of an egg, and gently blow out contents. Use skewer to hold shell while working. Paint shell with sizing; let set 15 minutes. While sizing is still tacky, apply mica powder with artist's brush, working over container to catch excess. (Wear a dust mask when working with mica powder.)
2. Place rubber band around middle of shell as a guide, and use pointed brush dipped in paint to apply designs. Glue foil-paper trim and beads on each end of egg. Affix beads with model cement. Thread gold cord through top bead to hang.

GRAPE CLUSTER WREATH

TOOLS AND MATERIALS *18- and 24-gauge brass wire; round-nose pliers; small round ornaments in graduated sizes, ranging between ⅝ and 1¾ inches in diameter; wire cutters; wide gold ribbon*

1. Use pliers to make a loop of one end of an 18-inch length of 18-gauge wire, forming stem of grape cluster. Insert a 26-inch length of 24-gauge wire through loop, and wrap to secure. Thread one of the smallest ornaments onto stem; wrap thinner wire around stem to secure. Repeat, adding about ten more of the smallest ornaments, wrapping with wire after each addition.
2. Next, add more of the smallest ornaments using extensions to enhance the cluster shape. Thread 5 inches of 24-gauge wire onto ornament hanger. Twist wire back upon itself to secure; trim excess. Using pliers, make a loop in end of wire (loop should be ½ to ¾ inch from hanger). String ornament onto stem through loop (you can also attach two ornaments to one extension). Continue adding ornaments, increasing in size until about two-thirds of the way up stem, and then decreasing in size toward the top of the cluster. When increasing in size, first add some ornaments without extensions, and then more of the same size with extensions. When decreasing in size, add ornaments with extensions first, and then more without. To hang, make a loop in stem about 1 inch from top of cluster. Tie a bow with ribbon, and drape over the top, attaching it to the nail.

CHAPTER three

A HOLIDAY BUFFET *of* SOUTHWESTERN FAVORITES

N*o matter where you live, you're likely* to have been taught as a child to sing "Let It Snow!" at Christmastime. The holiday, however, arrives in quite a few landscapes that rarely see snow. Its traditions in warmer climes may not center on snowball fights or sleigh rides, but they inspire the same feeling of nostalgia every December. The Garlands of Sedona, Arizona, often spend their holidays at Garland's Oak Creek Lodge, which the family has owned and operated for more than three decades. With the rooms closed to guests during the winter, the Garlands' lodge is the ideal place for everyone to gather. Over the years the family members have spent enough joyous Noels in their rusty-red desert habitat to prefer it over a white landscape every time.

For the Garlands, and lots of other families, the holiday season means big gatherings, which are both casual affairs and cooperative projects. Everyone pitches in to help prepare food and ready the lodge for the festivities. Faithful to the style established by Susan Garland and perfected by Amanda Stine (lodge chef for the past twenty-three years), the food is best described as homegrown American, with a focus on local ingredients and regional specialties. Meals are plentiful, but the presentation is easy, never fussy; rustic buffet tables are arranged with big platters

HOT, SPICY, AND SMOKY
Opposite: This spread features regional fare such as tamales, guacamole, two kinds of beans, cornbread, and a rack of venison with a jalapeño confit. A wreath of pepperberries and chiles plays off the menu. This page, from left: Horseback riders create a dusty trail in Oak Creek Canyon. Susan Garland, and her mother, Georgiana Isham Garland, share a laugh.

and bowls so everyone can help herself. With a nod to traditional holiday parties in nearby Mexico, the menu often includes tamales, which reflect the spirit of Christmas—unwrapping the husk is like opening a present. Cornhusks are also used for the party decorations. They're cut and crafted into delicate flowers—cosmos, daisies, apple blossoms, and sunflowers—then arranged in mixed bouquets, or bound together to make wreaths and napkin rings.

When Bill and Georgiana Garland took over the lodge in 1972, the whole family was enlisted to help, with each member assigned a particular task. Of Bill and Georgiana's children and children-in-law, only their son Gary and his wife, Mary, are still involved in running the establishment today. Family traditions remain unchanged, however. In fact, if a loud holler could sweep a ten-mile radius, it would pull in the whole gang, all sixteen of them. In a nation of families scattered hither and yon, such proximity is rare, but even more telling is the Garlands' enthusiasm for celebrating occasions *en famille*.

True to their name, they are a tight-knit and festive bunch. After dinner, dessert and Mexican hot chocolate are served, often around a campfire. Then some family members head back inside to sing old-time tunes around the player piano, and play card games such as P-I-G. Others opt instead to head out into the canyon for a little cool air and contemplation. The stars are big and bright, and the breeze in the canyon carries the lovely scent of ponderosa pines—perfect for a holiday celebration, with or without snow.

AT HOME IN THE CANYON
Opposite, clockwise from far left: Well-worn cowboy boots are appropriate attire for almost any occasion in the Southwest. Surrounding Nora, an Akita, are (from left) family friend Leslie Leonetti, Tricia Garland, Laurel Leonetti, Mary Garland, and Susan Garland. Medicine wheels such as this one in Long Canyon are very common in the Sedona area. When it's time for dessert, everyone will move outside to a fire pit sheltered by a grove of Douglas firs. A young Garland carefully balances eggs gathered from the henhouse. This page, clockwise from center left: Bill Garland's deep knowledge of Arizona history feeds many a story. A prickly pear cactus. A stoneware pitcher holds flowers fashioned from the husks of dried Indian corn. Georgiana and Bill take a break from the party to sit for a spell on the steps of Cabin Two. Georgiana and grandson Kevin work together to roll pastry dough. An agave plant, close up.

menu GUACAMOLE *with corn chips* * SPICE-RUBBED ROASTED RACK OF VENISON *with four-onion and jalapeño confit* * ASSORTED TAMALES * CHRISTMAS CORNBREAD STEWED FRIJOLES * GREEN BEANS AND CHAYOTE *with toasted pine nuts* * MEXICAN HOT CHOCOLATE * BISCOCHITOS * RICH CHOCOLATE TART * PASTEL DE TRES LECHES

PUTTING IT ALL TOGETHER

Opposite: Three shades of cornhusk apple blossoms adorn rustic napkin rings assembled with wire and floral tape. This page: Bold flavors and spices rule in the cuisine of the lodge, and the Garland family. At the table, a plate full of spice-rubbed venison, a cheese tamale, and all the Southwestern trimmings.

tamales: a Christmas tradition

TAMALE TIME *This page, top left: Classic ingredients for tamales include (clockwise from top left) cornhusks, banana leaves, batter, dried chiles, dried avocado leaves, fresh lard (solid vegetable shortening can also be used), and masa harina. Opposite: Tamales can be topped with (from left) sour cream, tomato-serrano salsa, and tomatillo-chipotle salsa. A black-bean tamale (center) resembles those from the Mexican state of Oaxaca.*

MAKING TAMALES

Christmas parties in Mexico aren't about just any food—they're about tamales, which are often served at *posadas*, the informal, piñata-breaking festivals celebrated throughout the nine days leading up to Christmas Eve. Tamales are always best right out of the steamer, but if you have leftovers, you can wrap them in plastic and refrigerate them for several days. To reheat, steam tamales 20 minutes. You can also freeze them up to 1 month, and steam 30 minutes to reheat.

SOAK THE CORNHUSKS

1. Dried cornhusks need to be reconstituted so they are pliable enough to work with. First, place them in a deep saucepan, and cover with water. Bring to a boil over high heat. Transfer the husks and the water to a heatproof bowl. Set a small plate on top of the husks, keeping them submerged. Soak 1 hour.

MAKE THE FILLINGS

2. Most recipes (ours start on page 116) call for tamale batter (shown here in a wooden spoon) as well as fillings, including (from top) black beans, buttery corn, and red-chile-seasoned pork.

ASSEMBLE THE TAMALES

3. Remove the husks from the water. Unroll one large piece, and tear it lengthwise along the grain to make ¼-inch-wide strips (you'll need two strips for each tamale); if strips aren't long enough, tie two together. Remove another large piece; lightly dry with a clean kitchen towel. Place on work surface, pointed end to one side; scoop ¼ cup batter onto middle of opposite end. Spread into a 4-inch square, leaving a 1½-inch border on pointed end and a 1-inch border on other sides. Spoon 2 tablespoons filling down the center. Pick up two long sides of the husk so the batter encases the filling. Bring two sides together, forming a cylinder. Fold pointed end under; tie loosely with a husk strip. Fold flat end under; tie with second strip.

PREPARE THE STEAMER

You can steam tamales in a bamboo steamer, a metal steamer basket, or a *tamalera*, a Mexican device resembling a divided bucket, made especially for steaming tamales.

4. If using a bamboo steamer, fill a wok with 2 inches of water. Line the bottom of steamer baskets with small cornhusks, and set baskets in place. Lay the assembled tamales in the steamer.

5. If you're using a *tamalera*, fill bottom with water, and insert plate. Line plate with cornhusks, and install the divider. Stand tamales vertically in the divided compartments (you'll only need to tie the flat ends shut; leave pointed ends open, and place the tied ends down). Layer more cornhusks on top, and cover.

STEAM THE TAMALES

Set steamer or *tamalera* over high heat. When steam puffs out, reduce heat to medium. Steam 1 hour 15 minutes, adding more water as necessary. To check for doneness, unwrap a tamale: If ready, the dough will come free from the wrapper and feel soft. If dough sticks to wrapper, rewrap tamale, and steam 15 to 20 minutes more. Remove from heat; let stand 15 minutes for batter to firm up. Tamales will remain warm for about 1 hour.

AFTER PARTY *This page, left: Pastel de tres leches, Spanish for "cake of three milks" is a dessert made for special occasions throughout the Southwest and in Mexico. When the butter-and-egg-rich sponge cake comes out of the oven, a mixture of whole and evaporated milks is poured over it; as they cool, cake and milk meld into a puddinglike delicacy. Right: A rich chocolate tart makes a nice counterpart to the tropical-fruit-garnished pastel de tres leches. The tart is the creation of Oak Creek Lodge chef Amanda Stine's. Opposite: Mexican hot chocolate, made with cinnamon, is served with dollops of rich whipped cream and anise-flavored Mexican sugar cookies called biscochitos.*

BEAUTIFUL BLOSSOMS
Multicolored ears of Indian corn abound at farm stands throughout the fall. Save some for projects such as this sunflower wreath. The husks are sold on their own at crafts stores.

projects CORNHUSK FLOWER WREATH * BOUQUETS * NAPKIN RINGS

GETTING STARTED *Cornhusks are naturally off-white or purple. To make pink husks, soak purple and off-white husks together in a bowl of water overnight. Before using dried husks for projects, soak them in water for 2 to 3 minutes; blot dry with paper towels. Copy templates (see page 136) onto card stock. Cut out, and place template on slightly damp husk with grain running in correct direction, then cut out shapes. Using your fingers, cup and shape petals while they dry.*

MAKING SUNFLOWER BLOSSOMS

TOOLS AND MATERIALS *cornhusks; card stock (for base and templates); scissors; dried corn kernels or popcorn; butter knife; clear varnish spray; tweezers; hot-glue gun; templates (page 136)*

For each flower, cut a 4-inch square of heavy red or orange card stock. Pry kernels from the cob with knife. Seal kernels with varnish before using to discourage weevils. Use tweezers to pick up a kernel of corn; dab with hot glue, and attach to center of card stock. Repeat, arranging glued kernels in pattern indicated in diagram below. Continue to add rows of kernels until flower center is desired size, between 2 and 3 inches

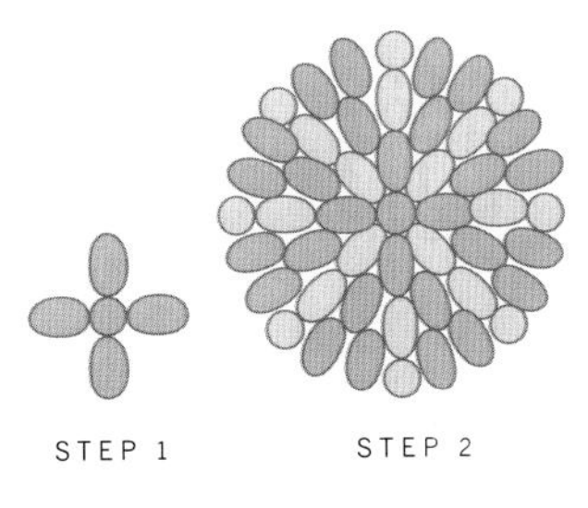

across; cut out. Next, accordion-fold several damp cornhusks. Place petal template on a folded husk, and cut out to produce several petals at a time. Repeat to make 45 to 50 petals of desired size (use small-petal template for a 2-inch center and large template for a 3-inch center). Hot-glue petals, one at a time, onto back of center disk, making 3 staggered rows so petals overlap. To make the wreath (opposite): Hot-glue eight flowers to a cardboard wreath form.

ATTACHING THE STEM

TOOLS AND MATERIALS *cornhusks; 18-gauge wire; scissors; 1/4-inch-diameter wooden dowel; white floral tape; hot-glue gun; card stock; template (page 136)*

Cut a 10-inch length of wire and bend it in half, forming a 1-inch loop at top. Bend wire gently just below loop to make flower's neck.

1. Attach wire to the end of the wooden dowel, about 3 inches from the loop, and secure with floral tape. Hot-glue the loop to back of flower disk. Accordion-fold several cornhusks. Place calyx-petal template on a folded husk, and cut out to produce several petals. Repeat to make 15 to 20 petals.

2. Hot-glue petals to back of disk, in staggered rows, covering entire back from flower to top of dowel. Trim dowel to desired stem length. Cut 1-inch-wide strips of husk. Wrap stem with strips: Hot-glue one end to top of dowel, where petals end, wrap, and hot-glue at other end. Repeat until stem is covered.

COSMOS AND DAISIES

TOOLS AND MATERIALS

cornhusks; templates (page 136); card stock; scissors; 18- and 32-gauge wire; pinking shears; dried corn kernels or popcorn; butter knife; clear varnish spray; white glue; small paintbrush; tweezers; brown floral tape

These blossoms can have either fringed or corn-kernel centers.

1. Using templates, cut out stamens (there is one template for each cosmos and two for each daisy). To make fringed stamens, fold strips along dotted line, then fringe one side with scissors. For cosmos, roll up stamen tightly, then wrap twice with the end of a 3-foot length of 32-gauge wire. For daisies, roll up inner stamen, and wrap twice with wire; roll outer stamen around that, and wrap with wire again.

2. Fold a still damp cornhusk accordion-style; place petal template on top, and cut out to produce several petals, making sure grain runs vertically. Repeat to make desired number of daisy and cosmos petals. Edge the top of each cosmos petal individually with pinking shears. Attach petals to stamen, wrapping twice with wire each time.

3. For corn-kernel flower centers, pry kernels from the cob with a butter knife. Seal kernels with varnish spray first to discourage weevils. To make unfringed stamens, fold cosmos stamen in half lengthwise (for daisies, use only inner stamen). Using white glue, affix several kernels with tweezers to center after attaching petals. Insert a length of 18-gauge wire through stamen base, securing with remaining 32-gauge wire; trim stem to desired length, and wrap with floral tape to finish.

To protect your decorations when storing, wrap them in acid-free tissue paper and enclose in a cardboard box. Though cornhusk flowers will never wilt, their colors may fade slightly if they are displayed year-round.

NAPKIN RINGS

TOOLS AND MATERIALS
cornhusks in off-white, purple, and pink; templates (page 136); card stock; scissors; 32-gauge wire; brown floral tape

For each napkin ring you will need five blossoms and several buds.

1. Using template, cut out blossom center, and fold along dotted line. Roll tightly to form stamen, wrapping twice with a 3-foot length of wire. Accordion-fold a cornhusk. Place petal template on top of folded husk, and cut out to produce several petals. Repeat with additional cornhusks to make more petals. Attach five petals around stamen, wrapping twice with wire each time. Cut out bud from template, and roll lengthwise. Wrap with another length of wire, two-thirds down roll. Open top of husk, fold down halfway, and wrap on itself; wire again.

2. To form napkin rings, wrap floral tape from base of each blossom and bud, 2 inches down stem. Cluster blossoms and buds, one at a time, securing wires together with floral tape. Bend wire into a 2-inch diameter ring, and trim ends. Push end into top of cluster to close loop.

1 2

IN GOOD COMPANY

Opposite: For the holidays, shrimp cocktail makes a celebratory starter. The shrimp can be cooked a day ahead then chilled. Sheila serves them with wedges of ripe avocado and whole basil leaves. Individual cups of cocktail sauce and lemon aïoli are set on each plate. This page, clockwise from top left: Angela Gubler, an art director, helped Sheila decorate, and brought along her 3-month-old daughter, Charlotte, to everyone's delight. Giant garlic croutons, brushed with olive oil and sprinkled with chopped parsley before toasting, accompany a salad of mixed greens that Jamie Prokell brings to the table. Sheila and work friends John Dunn and Jamie enjoy the meal—and the conversation. Just before serving time, John carved the roast, while Jamie filled glasses with wine.

menu SHRIMP COCKTAIL * FRISEE AND BIBB SALAD *with garlic croutons* ROASTED TENDERLOIN AU POIVRE * HARICOTS VERTS *with hazelnuts* * SMASHED RED POTATOES * PISTACHIO-CHOCOLATE BUCHE DE NOEL * VANILLA-BEAN BUTTER COOKIES

THE MAIN EVENT

This page: Despite its elegance, a roasted tenderloin, garnished with branches of fresh rosemary, isn't difficult to prepare. Opposite: Side dishes include green beans with toasted hazelnuts, and smashed red potatoes—quicker than mashed, they are made with a wire whisk instead of a mixer.

EASY DOES IT *Above, left to right: The main course gets the host's (and guests') approval. After the meal, Sheila leads the way to the living room for cookies and coffee. Opposite: Most of the menu's preparation was uncomplicated, but Sheila wanted to serve something for dessert that would leave everyone speechless—a bûche de Noël filled with pistachio ice cream and covered with sheets of chocolate "wood grain." A painter's tool covered in melted white chocolate is used to create the "knots" in the surface. As a garnish, chocolate leaves are made by painting melted chocolate onto real leaves.*

projects CEDAR AND PINECONE WREATH * EVERGREEN AND AMARYLLIS CENTERPIECES

CEDAR AND PINECONE WREATH

TOOLS AND MATERIALS

Square wire wreath form; branches of cedar or another evergreen; floral shears; 24-gauge floral wire on a paddle; pinecones; 4-inch-wide satin ribbon

A wreath is transformed when it's made on an oversize square form instead of the expected round type. **1.** Cut branches into sprigs 4 to 5 inches long; gather into bunches of four or five stems and secure at base with floral wire. Secure wire on paddle to the wreath form. Lay first bunch of sprigs on the form and wrap wire tightly three times around to secure branches to frame. Do not cut wire. Add another bunch of sprigs, overlapping previous one by half; wrap wire around stems. Continue adding bunches in the same direction until you reach the starting point. Tie wire under form, secure with a knot, and cut. Fill in any bare spots with more sprigs, if necessary. **2.** Cut an 18-inch piece of wire for each pinecone. Center a pinecone on a piece of wire and wrap wire around cone; attach pinecone to wreath by wrapping both ends of wire around wreath, then twisting ends to secure in back. Cut excess wire with floral shears. Repeat with more pinecones, placing them a few inches apart. Finish by wrapping satin ribbon around the top of the wreath, and tying a knot.

EVERGREEN CENTERPIECES

TOOLS AND MATERIALS

Evergreen cuttings, such as juniper; amaryllis blossoms; floral foam; large and small vases; floral shears; 24-gauge floral wire; small pinecones

Place a piece of floral foam inside each large vase. Cut evergreen stems to desired length (ours are approximately 3½ inches long). Stick stems into floral foam. Wrap wire around base of pinecones; trim wire to desired length to form "stems." Fill in arrangement with pinecones. Place vases filled with evergreens and pinecones alongside smaller vases with amaryllis blooms. Spritzing the greenery periodically with water will keep it moist and fresh for several days.

CHAPTER five

AN OPEN HOUSE *on* CHRISTMAS DAY

A *spirit of generosity prevails at* Christmastime, and there's hardly a better way to spread the good feeling than opening your home to friends and neighbors. Every December 25 across the country (and in many other parts of the world), open houses are held, from formal events with fancy fare served in the family heirloom silver and crystal to more casual get-togethers where guests in jeans arrive bearing favorite potluck dishes. The point of these parties is to offer visitors the last gift of the year—a bountiful supply of good food and good company—and to give everyone time to relax as they catch up on how life has unfolded during the previous twelve months.

Such is the kind of party that Arthur Kahn, a wine retailer in Memphis, and his wife, Lisa Mallory, an interior decorator, have in mind when they host an annual gathering at their country place in New England. Located at the edge of a Vermont wood, the 220-year-old home has a history of entertaining. In the nineteenth century, it was a public house, the comings and goings innumerable; in the early twentieth century, it operated as a tearoom. Today, it makes an ideal if unexpected setting for this family of five to showcase their Southern hospitality. Their party can serve as a model for any holiday open house. The

THROUGH THE WOODS
Opposite: Garlands of greenery and big glass lanterns on the porch help set the house apart from the stark white landscape. This page, from left: A delicious-looking though inedible bird "cookie" ornament surveys the festivities from its lookout on the Christmas tree. All afternoon, neighbors and friends, some with covered dishes in hand, come and go via the snowy country road.

decorations are from nature, or mimic it. Christmas greenery is swirled around the columns on the front porch, shaped into an unusual straight wreath for the door, wound among candlesticks on the mantel in the living room, even tucked below the mirrored sconces in the entryway. The tree is the biggest presence from outdoors, of course. Along with its glass ornaments are decorations drawing from nature as well—whimsical, cinnamon-scented, sparkle-feathered birds that look and smell like cookies but, being made with glue, are meant to stay on the tree, not land on the dessert table.

As for the edible part of the proceedings, most of the food is made the day before, so the hosts are able to spend unhurried time with their guests. Arthur and Lisa choose dishes that can be enjoyed at room temperature, such as ham and roasted turkey breast, allowing for greater flexibility in planning the menu. And since everything is on offer for several hours, the hosts make sure to keep plenty on hand to replenish the buffet as the sun starts to set. A second stuffed turkey breast, for example, goes into the oven after the first one comes out. Biscuits are baked in advance and frozen and pans of thawed biscuits are popped into the oven for reheating throughout the day. Sweets, including cookies, rum balls, and a pear tart, all hold up well.

Guests often leave long after darkness has fallen, but their spirits are light as they find their way back home through the still, snow-covered woods.

COMINGS AND GOINGS
Opposite, from left: Son Richard (left) and a friend keep the home fires burning with regular trips to the woodpile. The living room's bright fire and tree sparkling with ornaments welcome guests in from the cold. This page, left to right, top to bottom: On the day before the party, daughters Nora and Zoë dip fresh pears, apples, and citrus fruits in hot wax; once cool, the waxed fruit shines among evergreen branches placed on the windowsills and atop the mantel. Dessert wine makes a smooth accompaniment to a slice of pear tart. Red wine is poured and set out with an assortment of cheeses and crackers. Richard savors the anticipation of opening a stack of brightly wrapped gifts. The family keeps several horses in the property's stable. Hostess Lisa Mallory finds a spot on the tree for a feathered friend. Nora greets a guest arriving with more treats for the family.

menu CRANBERRY-CITRUS PUNCH * ROASTED ALMONDS *with olive oil*
CROSTINI *with smoked trout* * ROASTED TURKEY BREAST *with fennel-herb stuffing*
SMOKED HAM *with maple glaze* * GRAPEFRUIT AND CRANBERRY CHUTNEY
BUTTERNUT SQUASH CRUMBLE * GREEN BEANS *with shiitake mushrooms*
GREEN SALAD *with walnuts and date vinaigrette* * CHEDDAR CHEESE AND SAGE BISCUITS

FESTIVE EDIBLES *This page, from left: Smoked-trout spread tops a crostini wreath, with red and green vegetables used as garnish; cranberry-citrus punch can be served with or without Champagne. Hors d'oeuvres await visitors by the door. Opposite: Fresh bay leaves, kumquats, and orange votive candles make a fresh, nontraditional centerpiece for the all-day buffet.*

YOURS FOR THE TAKING

Opposite: Among the array of dishes to choose from are two main courses—a butterflied turkey breast rolled around fennel-herb stuffing, and, with a nod to the state of Vermont, maple-syrup-glazed smoked ham. This page: Served with dessert, sweet wines such as Sauternes make a festive alternative to coffee.

desserts RUM BALLS * GINGER CHEESECAKE BARS
MAPLE SHORTBREAD *with pecans* * COCONUT-CRANBERRY COOKIES * PEAR TART

SWEET OFFERINGS *Above left: The filling and crust of this pear tart are flavored with almonds. Vanilla-bean crème anglaise is served in a bowl alongside, so guests can spoon out as much or as little as they like. Right: In the kitchen, Lisa opens a home-baked gift brought by a neighbor and kept warm wrapped in a dish towel during the trip over. On the counter is a freshly heated batch of biscuits.*

LAYERED DELIGHTS *Above left: Rich rum balls, coated in sparkling red sanding sugar, crown a three-tiered dessert tray that includes ginger-flavored cheesecake bars and two kinds of cookies: maple shortbread with pecans and coconut-cranberry. Right: Zoë, donning a Christmas-red blouse and a holiday smile, knows first-hand how good the desserts are, and makes herself a plate with a sampling.*

projects BOXWOOD *and* FRUIT STRAIGHT WREATH

ORANGE VOTIVES * WAXED FRUIT * FAUX-GINGERBREAD ORNAMENTS

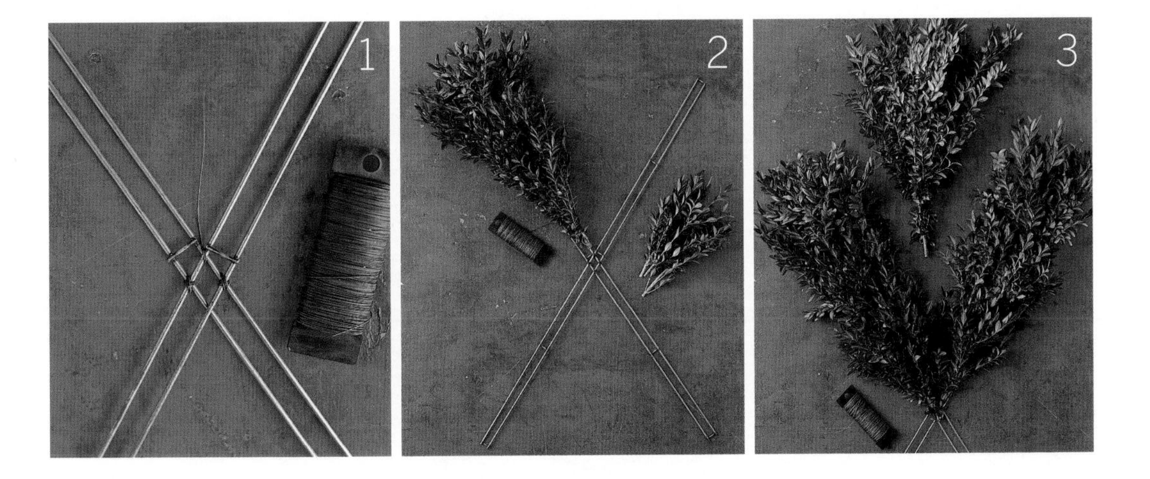

STRAIGHT WREATH

TOOLS AND MATERIALS

*two 24-inch straight metal wreath frames; 24-gauge wire; multipurpose shears; boxwood; lady apples; oranges; toothpicks; strawberry tree (*Arbutus unedo*) sprigs*

This untraditional wreath of boxwood, oranges, and lady apples welcomes visitors at Lisa Mallory and Arthur Kahn's front door. The cold winter air ensures that the fruit will stay vibrant for a few weeks.

1. Cross two straight metal wreath frames to make an X; secure them to each other with wire at the four points where they overlap.

2. Make bundles of boxwood by tightly wrapping wire around four or five stalks. Wire a bundle onto form, starting at top of one leg of X. Repeat, making sure top of next bundle overlaps stems of previous one, until top half of form is covered.

3. Wire several more bundles together to create a section to fit between the top of the X; wire this to the center of the form, and fill small gaps with more boxwood. Repeat process for bottom of form. Thread lady apples onto a 1-foot length of wire, leaving 1 inch between entrance and exit points (pictured at right); twist at center, and use ends to secure to center of form. With a toothpick, pierce one side of each orange (they are too heavy to thread directly onto wire), leaving ¼ inch of toothpick exposed on either end (pictured at right). Tightly wrap an 18-inch length of wire around toothpick ends in a figure eight; twist at center, and secure to form with remaining ends. Wire strawberry tree sprigs to center of wreath.

ORANGE VOTIVES

TOOLS AND MATERIALS
navel oranges; sharp knife; saltcellars or other small bowls (to keep the orange rinds stable); tea-light holders; tea lights; 1¾-inch scalloped-edge cookie cutter (no smaller or flame will burn orange rind)

1. Slice an orange in half crosswise. Slide your fingers between the flesh and the skin to loosen and remove segments (set segments aside to make juice, if desired).
2. Set bottom rind of orange in a saltcellar, cut side up, and place a tea-light holder with tea light in the center. Place the top rind, cut side up, on a work surface, and mark its center with the knife (the stem may not indicate the exact center but should be part of the piece that is removed). Center cookie cutter over mark, and press down firmly to create a scalloped hole. Discard cutout. Place top half of rind on bottom half, making sure the hole is centered over the candle so the rind won't burn; adjust the tea light if necessary. Remove top to light candle, and carefully replace.

WAXED FRUIT, PINECONES, AND SEED PODS

TOOLS AND MATERIALS *2 to 3 pounds beeswax; slow cooker (with removable dishwasher-proof liner) or an inexpensive heatproof bowl (you will have to discard after using); fruit (up to 50 pieces, depending on size, of any of the following: kumquats, pears, apples, lady apples, grapefruit, pomelos); awl; waxed paper; pinecones and seed pods; 24-gauge wire*

1. Melt beeswax in slow cooker with liner, on high setting, or in the heatproof bowl set over a pot of water over low heat (2 pounds of wax will take about 45 minutes; use more if dipping many large fruits, such as pomelos). Keep warm on low heat. Starting with large pieces, to assure enough wax for even coverage, spear bottom of fruit with awl.
2. Quickly dip fruit in wax, twirl to coat, and remove, letting excess drip into pot. Hold until wax hardens, then slide fruit off awl, and place on waxed paper bottom side down. Let dry for 3 minutes. Insert awl again; dip fruit for a second coat.
3. Wrap wire around bottom of pinecones and pods; dip. These will need about six coats each. Pinecones and pods can be stored after the holidays and reused for several seasons; the fruit will keep for about 2 weeks.

WINTER WINDOWSILL
Nestled among branches of princess pine, waxed fruit shines in the sunlight. Beeswax works better than other types of wax because it is more pliable, so it won't crack or break.

GLITTER AND BEAD GLOSSARY

1. *pink powder glitter*
2. *red seed beads*
3. *two-millimeter silver-colored plastic-resin beads*
4. *copper glass glitter*
5. *gold plastic glitter*
6. *white plastic glitter*
7. *three-millimeter silver-colored plastic resin beads*
8. *green microbead glitter*

FLIGHTS OF FANCY *This flock of bird ornaments, which includes a cardinal, tanager, and chickadee, will migrate each winter, becoming decorations on the Christmas tree. Applesauce gives the dough pliability, glue makes it become firm, cinnamon imparts a lovely holiday fragrance, and glitter and beads add sparkle and color.*

FAUX-GINGERBREAD ORNAMENTS

TOOLS AND MATERIALS

1 cup ground cinnamon; 1/4 cup applesauce; rubber spatula; 1/2 cup white craft glue, plus more for decorating; parchment paper; rolling pin; utility knife; drinking straw; assorted glitter and beads (see glossary, opposite)

1. In a medium bowl, mix together the cinnamon and applesauce using the rubber spatula; stir in glue. Toss the dough over and over until the consistency is smooth and dry. Let dough stand 1 hour.

2. Turn out one-quarter of dough onto a cool, parchment-lined surface; flatten mound with your hands.

3. Roll out dough to ¼ inch thick. If it becomes too dry, spritz with water. If it sticks to rolling pin or work surface, sprinkle with cinnamon.

4. Lay a bird template (see page 137) over dough; cut out shapes with the utility knife (alternatively, use bird-shaped cookie cutters).

5. Repeat with three remaining quarters of dough. With straw, poke a hole in dough as indicated on template (for hanging ornament). Preheat oven to 200°F. Transfer ornaments to a baking sheet; bake, flipping once, until completely dry, about 2 hours. Alternatively, let ornaments air-dry on a wire rack lined with paper towels for 24 hours; flip every 6 hours to keep them flat.

6. Spread craft glue over the area of the bird that you wish to decorate.

7. While glue is still wet, hold ornament over a bowl of glitter or beads and spoon decoration over glue; tap off excess. As you decorate your birds, work from the finest embellishment to the coarsest, adding glitter then beads in order of size.

8. Wait for the first area to dry completely, at least 30 minutes, before repeating steps 6 and 7 on another section of the ornament. Once the ornaments are dried and decorated, they'll last for years.

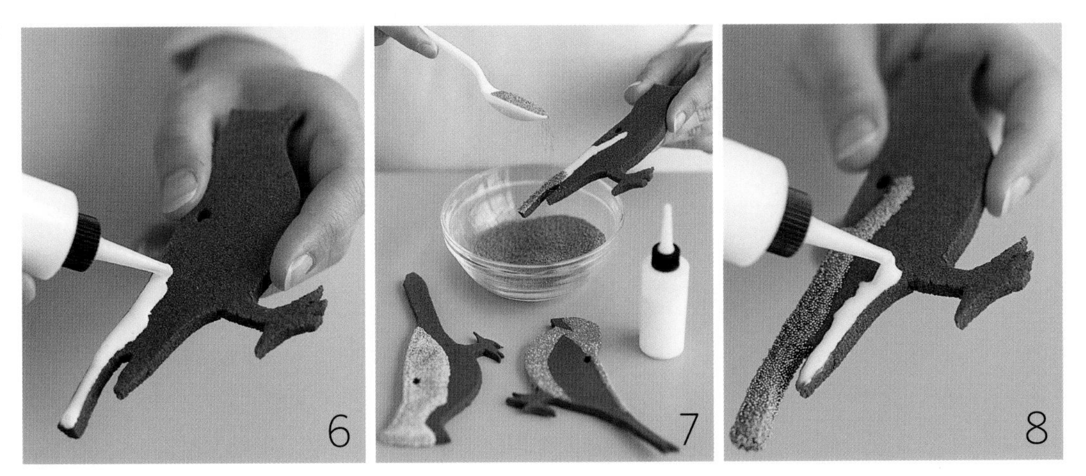

CHAPTER six

NEW YEAR'S EVE DINNER *in* THE CITY

E*very New Year's Eve, the ball-dropping ceremony in* Times Square is shown on television around the world. Crowds flock to Manhattan to catch the action live on the street, but many New Yorkers choose instead to seek refuge in a quiet apartment with a few close friends. For them, revving up for the stroke of midnight means taking it easy. That's where the kind of intimate dinner party Eric Pike likes to host on New Year's Eve fits in. Guests arrive in the afternoon and relax, even dawdle, in his winter-wondrous apartment while they sip Champagne and feast on an assortment of wonderful cheeses and caviar. Later on, Eric serves a light dinner—risotto followed by a salad—then offers everyone his favorite dessert, grasshopper tarts, and a chance to stay for the countdown, make their way to another party, or head home.

Executive creative director—and resident Jack Frost—of *Martha Stewart Living,* Eric decorates for the holiday season by bringing the glistening ice and snow of a fine winter's day inside without the chilly temperature. A little spray frost on windows, clocks, and other glass surfaces adds luster to the muted silvery greens of his décor, setting a convivial but elegant tone for the party. Commemorated with a lovely, laid-back day and night, the old year slips gently into the new.

FROSTY FETE *Opposite: On the Christmas tree, shorter icicle ornaments hang toward the top, longer ones toward the bottom, to mimic the way ice forms on trees outdoors. A silvered square boxwood wreath is hung from fishing line so it appears to float in the window. Above, from left: A Gustavian clock seems frozen in time, but it is actually just decorated with easy-to-remove spray frost. Trumpet ornaments are also embellished with spray frost and given as party favors.*

CRYSTAL PERSUASION

Opposite: An antique mirror appears icy without help from nature or manmade spray frost; it is draped with varying lengths of glass icicles individually strung on short pieces of thin wire then twisted onto a tinsel garland. A phalaenopsis orchid is placed in front of the mirror. This page, clockwise from above left: On an antique Swedish desk turned sideboard, candles in frosted hurricanes cast a glow over a store-bought buffet of cheeses, assorted crackers, caviar, and blini (for a glossary of Eric's favorite cheeses, see page 131; for a caviar glossary, see page 132); Lucite pedestals under the candles and serving dishes call to mind sheets of ice; hypericum berries in silver-lustre compotes add cheer. A café au lait bowl filled with moss catches light filtered through an "icy" windowpane. A guest spreads a raisin-studded cracker with creamy Humboldt Fog cheese.

BRIGHT LIGHT, BIG CITY

Opposite: At a table set with pale linens, the clean lines of Swedish chairs provide striking contrast to the airy feel of the dining room. Eric's floors are painted a cool shade of gray, which contributes to the wintry scene. Round boxwood wreaths, dusted with metallic floral sprays, contrast nicely with square wreaths in the living room. New Lametta tinsel garlands are strung with glass beads from vintage Christmas garlands—fun to search for in flea markets and antiques shops all year. This page, clockwise from top left: Eric fills flutes with Champagne for his guests. A square vase adorned with spray frost holds two of Eric's favorite flowers, hellebores and amaryllis, in chartreuse and other shades of green. "Ice" forms on the panes of this glass-front cabinet with the press of a button on a can of spray frost.

menu ASSORTED CHEESES AND CAVIAR * SHRIMP AND GREEN PEA RISOTTO
ROASTED PEAR AND SHALLOT SALAD *with sherry-Dijon vinaigrette* * GRASSHOPPER TARTS

FRUITS OF THE TABLE *Opposite: A salad featuring roasted pears and shallots takes delectable advantage of available winter fruits and vegetables. Above left: Throughout the apartment, Eric's Lucite pedestals make food and decorations seem as if they are resting atop blocks of ice. Votive candles glow more intensely than usual as their light bounces off the many reflective surfaces on the table. Above right: Risotto is the host's entrée of choice for a small dinner party because it is at once sophisticated, satisfying, and easy to make. "Just prep and stir," he says. This shrimp-and-green-pea version is brightened by the addition of parsley and lemon zest.*

COOL HOSPITALITY *Opposite: A store-bought dessert buffet featuring meringues, macaroons, assorted butter cookies, and marzipan pears is arranged on a tea table beneath a hanging glass cabinet. Behind the cabinet's frosted windows, Eric's impressive collection of mercury-glass vases shines. This page, from left: Eric's friends Shawn Chavez and Sarina Vetterli prepare to indulge in individual grasshopper tarts. Flavored with crème de menthe and chilled in chocolate wafer crusts, this dessert has been enjoyed by the host since he was a child. "I love the combination of mint and chocolate," he says. The tartlets are simply garnished with chocolate shavings and brought to the table together on a footed glass cake stand.*

LANDSCAPE IN MINIATURE *On top of a bookcase, icicle ornaments drip from real branches dusted with silver glitter. Although not airtight, glass laboratory funnels placed over bowls of moss create a terrarium atmosphere; the moss is spritzed now and then to keep it healthy. The deer figurines are made of mercury glass.*

projects DECORATING WITH SPRAY FROST
SILVERED WREATH ✴ GLITTERED BRANCHES

DECORATING WITH SPRAY FROST

TOOLS AND MATERIALS *Spray frost; masking tape and paper to protect areas not to be frosted*

For best results, apply spray frost to clean, smooth, nonporous surfaces that are either transparent (such as windows or glass cabinets) or that reflect light (such as mirrors); follow the manufacturer's instructions carefully, and be sure to work in a well-ventilated area. For a windowed cabinet (above left), start at the top, working on one pane at a time. Tape paper over the surrounding trim and glass as you work, to protect them from excess spray. Aim the nozzle where you want to position the top curved edge of the frost (above right), holding the can about 15 inches from the surface. Move your hand from side to side in a gentle sweeping motion as you spray. Repeat as needed, filling in any sparse areas near the bottom of the pane. To "thaw" the frost after the holidays, simply wipe it away with a paper towel and warm water.

SILVERED WREATH

TOOLS AND MATERIALS
Boxwood branches; floral wire; square or round wreath form; gold and silver floral spray

Cut boxwood branches to 5-inch lengths. Gather branches into bunches; secure them at their bases with floral wire. Using wire, attach bunches to wreath form (overlapping each bunch) until entire frame is covered. Lightly mist wreath with gold floral spray, then with a thin layer of silver floral spray.

GLITTERED BRANCHES

TOOLS AND MATERIALS
Paper to cover work surface; paintbrush; white glue; branches; dust mask; clear glass glitter; vase or jar; white plastic beads

Cover your work surface with paper that you can fold up carefully and dispose of after you have completed the project. Paint glue onto bare branches. Wearing mask, sprinkle glass glitter over the glue. When completely dry, place the branches in a vase or jar partially filled with white plastic beads to look as if they're poking up out of snow.

CHAPTER seven

A JAPANESE LUNCH *with* GOOD WISHES *for the* NEW YEAR

B*elieving the first of January to be the most auspicious* day of the new year, the Japanese traditionally wake at dawn to greet the first sunrise (known as *hatsuhinode*). This is how a day meant to be spent joyfully begins. According to tradition, stress and anger must be banished; the peaceful orientation they leave behind is said to promise happiness for the rest of the year. No matter your heritage, the graceful optimism of these traditions is an excellent reason to throw a New Year's Day party, one whose express purpose is to shower good fortune on friends and family.

For this party, guests arrive with new year's wishes written on strips of origami paper that were mailed with the invitations. They then hang each wish on a garland—in this case, strung along the banister of the front staircase. The Christmas tree is trimmed with origami cranes (said to bring good luck) and fans. The menu features soba noodles, one of Japan's most beloved foods. In Japan, the noodles, which symbolize longevity, are eaten at midnight on New Year's Eve, when they are called *toshikoshi* ("from one year to another"). It's another fitting sentiment for a time filled with hope.

PEACE AND PLENTY
Opposite: The table is set beneath a paper chandelier; square cushions function as chairs. Soba noodles, made from buckwheat, are served in a yellowware bowl. Placing the bowl atop another inverted one turns a serving dish into a centerpiece. This page: A young partygoer shows off her origami crane.

TOKENS OF GOOD FORTUNE

Opposite: A garland of wishes brightens up the stairway. This page, top left: Party invitations include long strips of decorative paper. Guests will write their wishes for the new year on the strips, then tie them to the garland upon arriving. As the crowd grows, so does the number of wishes. Keep a stack of extra paper on hand so guests can write and add on as many wishes as they like. Top right: Favors filled with Japanese candies are wrapped in bags constructed of patterned rice paper. A tag is attached to each favor, marking it for a specific guest. Bottom: Rectangles of paper, folded accordion style into origami fans, decorate gifts placed under the tree for the younger guests.

menu BEEF NEGIMAKI *with asparagus* ✶ LONG-LIFE NOODLES SESAME TOFU *with miso glaze* ✶ JAPANESE SALAD *with watercress and bay scallops* GREEN-TEA GRANITA ✶ GREEN-TEA SHORTBREAD LEAVES

LUCKY NOODLES

In the Far East, soba noodles represent the wish for a long life, so the longer they are, the better. Don't break or cut them when cooking or serving. In this dish, sweet potato and daikon (winter radish) are shaved into long thin strands to echo the noodles' shape. Opposite: Beef negimaki, an hors d'oeuvre, is served with disposable chopsticks that are wrapped in red paper napkins and colorful origami paper.

SAVORY AND SWEET *This page, left: In Asian cooking, no protein is more versatile than tofu, a culinary chameleon that takes on the flavors of whatever seasonings it is prepared with. Sesame tofu with miso glaze is served on a bed of julienned scallions and paper-thin radishes. Right: A salad of watercress and bay scallops incorporates thinly sliced cucumbers for crunch. Opposite: Inspired by green-tea ice cream, a staple dessert in many Japanese restaurants in the United States, green-tea granita, made with powdered tea, sake, and sugar, is light and refreshing. Green-tea shortbread completes the dessert course.*

SYMBOLS OF HOPE

Trimming a tree with origami cranes and garlands of paper fans is a lovely way to honor the memory of a young girl named Sadako Sasaki. After she developed leukemia as a result of the 1945 Hiroshima bombing, Sadako learned of a legend that told if a person folded one thousand paper cranes, the gods might grant his or her wish. Sadako wanted to get well, but didn't finish making all of the cranes before she died. Her classmates, however, folded enough cranes to make up the difference. Since then, people the world over have sent thousands of folded cranes to Sadako's monument in Hiroshima. "Peace trees" are decorated in her memory in other parts of the world as well, including at the Cathedral Church of Saint John the Divine in New York City.

projects ORIGAMI CRANES ✱ FOLDED FANS ✱ GIFT BAGS

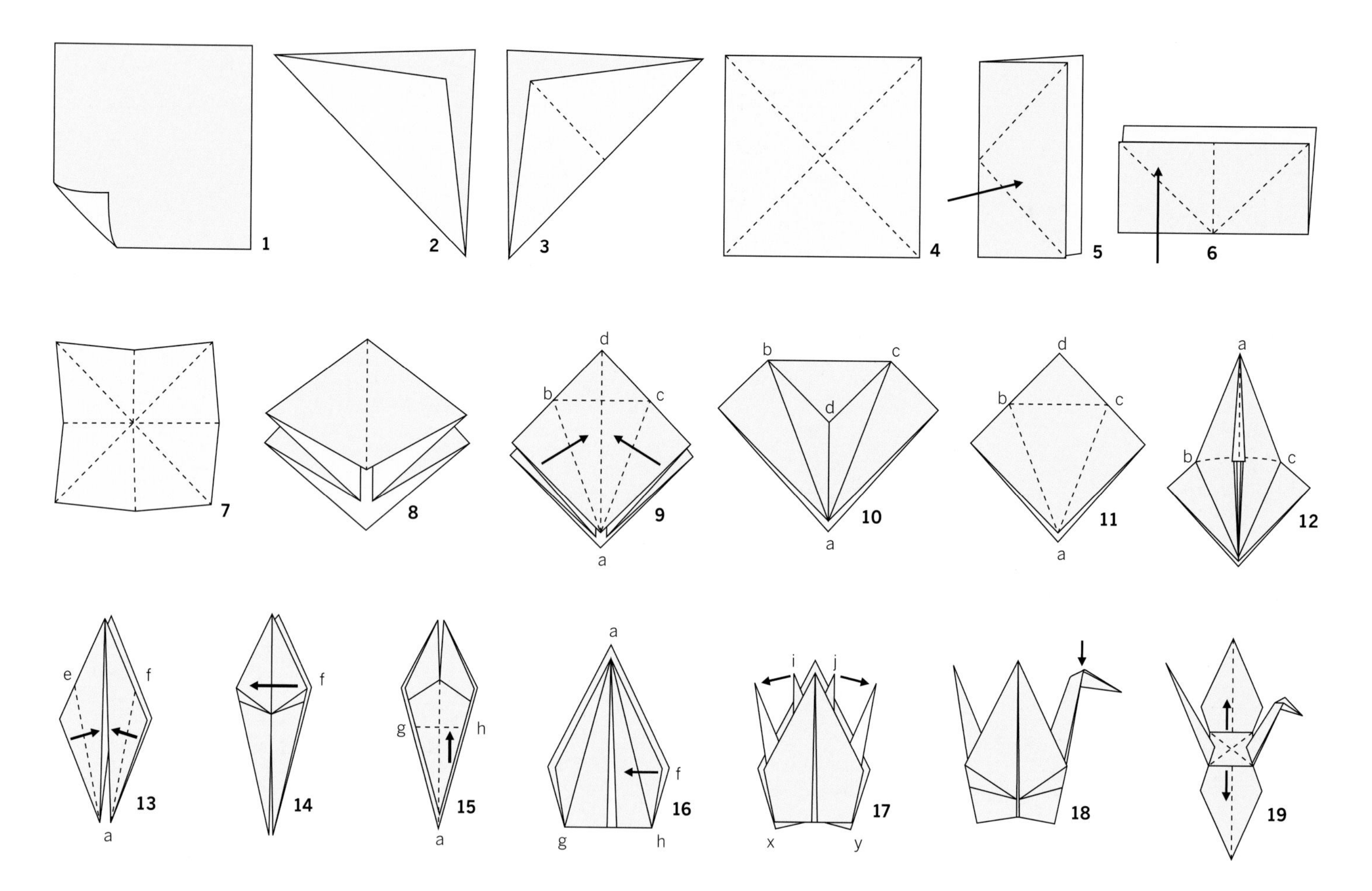

ORIGAMI CRANES

Folding a paper crane takes practice. As you work, be sure to make your creases sharp and to match corners and edges carefully.

1. Start with a square of origami paper that is colored on one side.

2. With the colored side facing up, fold the paper diagonally into a triangle. Crease well, and unfold.

3. Fold diagonally in the opposite direction. Crease well, and unfold.

4. Turn paper colored side down.

5. Fold in half vertically to form a rectangle. Crease well, and unfold.

6. Fold in half horizontally; crease.

7. Unfold, but don't flatten square.

8. Bring all four corners of the paper together, folding one at a time, until you have a flat square. (There will be one open end and two flaps on the left and right.)

9. Position open end at the bottom. Lift top flap on the right side, and fold toward the center, as arrow indicates. Crease along dotted line a–c. Repeat with top flap on left side, creasing along dotted line a–b.

10. Fold the top point (d) down along dotted line b–c, and crease.

11. Unfold the three folds you just made. Lift the top layer of paper at point a, and fold it back, creasing on the inside along dotted line b–c.

12. Press down on points b and c, smoothing sides of paper into a long, flat diamond shape. Flip paper over, and repeat steps 9, 10, and 11 on this side.

13. The folded paper should now look like a diamond with two "legs" at the bottom. Taper bottom (legs) of the diamond by folding the top layer of each to meet the center, along dotted lines a–e and a–f. Flip paper over; repeat tapering folds.

14. Lift the upper flap only at point f, and fold all the way over in the direction of the arrow, as if turning the page of a book. Flip the paper over, and repeat this "book" fold.

15. Lift the upper layer of the point at the bottom (point a) and fold it back so it meets with top points, creasing along dotted line g–h. Flip paper over; repeat on other side.

16. Lift top flap on right side at point f; fold over as if turning the page of a book. Flip paper over; repeat.

17. You will now see two points, i and j, beneath the top flap. Holding the bottom, pull each one outward, as shown, and then press down at points x and y to secure them in place.

18. Fold the end of one point downward to form the crane's head; reverse the crease in the head, and pinch to form the beak. The other point will be the crane's tail.

19. Pull wings outward and gently blow into the opening underneath the crane to fill out the body.

FOLDED FANS

TOOLS AND MATERIALS

Origami paper; bone folder; waxed twine; thin beading cord; large sewing needle

We used 4-by-8½-inch origami paper for large fans and 2½-by-6-inch paper for garlands. Crease paper by folding it in half crosswise, and then in half again. Repeat until paper is ¼ inch wide; smooth creases with bone folder as you go. Unfold. Accordion-fold, using creases as guides. Gather paper ¼ inch from bottom, and tie with twine. Poke a hole at top of fan; thread cord through with needle, and tie into a loop. To make garland, knot one end of cord, and stitch through one corner of fan with the needle. Run across back of fan, stitch through opposite corner, then continue with next fan. Note: Garlands longer than 3 feet will tangle.

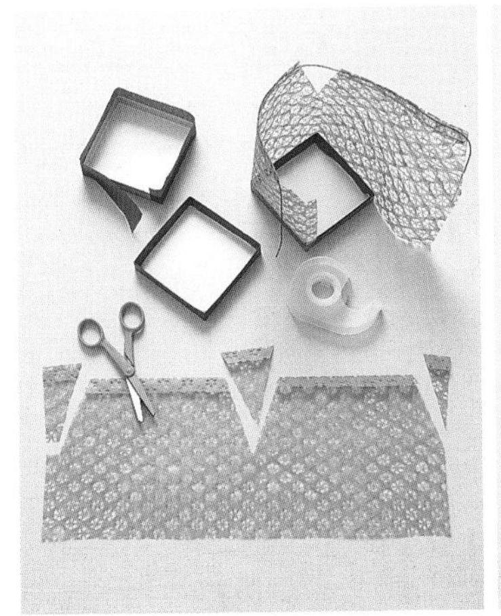

GIFT BAGS

TOOLS AND MATERIALS

gift boxes; double-sided tape; tissue paper; patterned rice paper; scissors; needle and thread or sewing machine; cord or ribbon; gift tags made from origami paper

Each of these presents uses only the top or bottom of a box. Position box open side up. Cover sides of box with a strip of double-sided tape. Wrap sides with a strip of colored tissue paper twice as tall as the sides. Fold excess tissue paper into the box. Cover tissue paper with another layer of double-sided tape. Set box aside. Cut a strip of rice paper ½ inch longer than the perimeter of box and to desired height. Fold down one long edge ¾ inch. Cut a notch in center of rice paper and slice off a wedge from sides, as shown above left. Sew folded edge into a channel. Affix opposite end of rice paper to sides of box, as shown above left. Seal seam with tape. Thread thin cord through channel. Wrap present in tissue and place inside. Slip a tag onto cord and cinch the bag, finishing with a bow.

TO MAKE VARIATIONS SHOWN AT RIGHT: Cut same-size pieces of tissue and rice paper, ½ inch longer than perimeter of box and to desired height. Tape the tissue paper to sides of box, add another layer of double-sided tape, then secure rice paper to box. Place present inside. Fold over the top, punch a hole in fold, and tie on tag with thin ribbon or cord, as shown, or simply cinch around middle with a gift tag and cord.

THE RECIPES

A FAMILY GATHERS AT HOME *for the* HOLIDAYS

CHEESE FONDUE

SERVES 8 TO 10

If your fondue is too thick, add more warmed cider or wine; if it is too thin, stir in a bit of cornstarch. If fondue separates and becomes lumpy, return pot to stove and gently whisk over moderate heat; mix some cornstarch with cider or wine, and stir into the fondue.

- 1 garlic clove, halved horizontally
- 1½ cups apple cider or dry white wine
- 8 ounces grated Gruyère cheese (about 3 cups)
- 8 ounces grated Emmental cheese (about 3 cups)
- 8 ounces grated raclette cheese (about 3 cups)
- 2 tablespoons freshly squeezed lemon juice
- 2 tablespoons cornstarch
- Freshly grated nutmeg
- Freshly ground white pepper
- 1 loaf French bread (1 pound), cut into 1-inch cubes
- Assorted pickled vegetables, such as cornichons, pearl onions, cauliflower florets, baby carrots, and mushrooms, for serving (optional)

1. Rub the inside of a fondue pot with the cut garlic clove; discard garlic. Pour cider into pot, and heat over low heat. When it begins to bubble, start adding cheeses a handful at a time, stirring until melted after each addition.

2. Whisk together lemon juice and cornstarch in a small bowl until cornstarch has dissolved. When all of the cheese has melted, stir into cheese mixture. Continue stirring until mixture is smooth and bubbling slightly, about 5 minutes. Season with nutmeg and white pepper.

3. Transfer fondue pot to table, and keep warm over a burner. Serve with bread and pickled vegetables, as desired.

ENDIVE AND RADISH SALAD

SERVES 8 TO 10

- 2 heads Bibb or Boston lettuce
- 6 heads Belgian endive, halved lengthwise and sliced crosswise into 1-inch pieces
- 1 small bunch radishes, trimmed and thinly sliced
- 1 bunch scallions, white and light-green parts only, thinly sliced
- 2 tablespoons freshly squeezed lemon juice
- 2 tablespoons extra-virgin olive oil
- Coarse salt and freshly ground pepper

Tear lettuce into bite-size pieces, and place in a large serving bowl. Add endive, radishes, and scallions. Drizzle with lemon juice and oil, and toss to combine. Season with salt and pepper. Serve immediately.

SMOKED HAM WITH HONEY-ORANGE GLAZE

SERVES 10 WITH LEFTOVERS

To carve the ham, begin by cutting out a small V-shaped piece of meat from the top near the hock end. From that point, cut ham into thin slices at a forty-five-degree angle on both sides of the V.

- 1 whole smoked ham (14 to 18 pounds), with bone and rind intact
- ½ cup honey
- ⅓ cup freshly squeezed orange juice
- 3 tablespoons balsamic vinegar
- 1 tablespoon Dijon mustard
- 1 large onion, peeled and cut into 6 wedges
- 1 large orange, peeled and cut into 6 wedges
- 4 sprigs rosemary
- ½ cup cider vinegar
- 3½ cups homemade or low-sodium store-bought chicken stock
- 3 tablespoons all-purpose flour
- Coarse salt and freshly ground pepper

1. Rinse ham with cool water, and pat dry with paper towels. Let stand at room temperature, uncovered, 1 hour. Meanwhile, whisk together honey, orange juice, balsamic vinegar, and mustard. Set glaze aside.

2. Preheat oven to 300°F, with rack in lower third. Fit a roasting pan with a rack. Transfer ham, with the thicker rind on top, to rack. Scatter onion and orange wedges and rosemary around pan. Cook 1 hour.

3. Remove ham from oven; let cool slightly. Raise oven temperature to 350°F. Trim fat to a ¼-inch layer all around ham (it does not need to be perfectly even, since the bottom will have less fat and more skin). Turn ham top side up. Score remaining fat on top with 1- to 2-inch diamonds, cutting about 1/4 inch into ham. Baste with some of the glaze. Add enough water to roasting pan to be 1/4 inch deep.

4. Return ham to oven; cook 1 hour more, basting often with remaining glaze. (Do not baste with pan juices. If necessary, add additional water to roasting pan to keep pan juices from burning.) Remove from oven; let cool slightly. Transfer to a serving platter, and let stand 30 minutes before carving.

5. While ham is resting, make the gravy: Strain liquid from roasting pan into a liquid measuring cup or bowl; with a large spoon, skim off fat that rises to the surface. Place roasting pan over medium-high heat. Add cider vinegar, and simmer until most of the liquid has evaporated. Return defatted juices to pan along with 2 cups chicken stock. Bring to a boil, then keep at a simmer. In a small bowl, whisk together remaining 1 1/2 cups stock with the flour until well combined. Whisk into sauce; continue simmering until liquid is reduced by half and somewhat thickened. Season with salt and pepper; transfer to a gravy boat, and serve hot with slices of ham.

VANILLA APPLESAUCE

SERVES 8 TO 10

Applesauce will keep in an airtight container in the refrigerator for up to three days.

- 14 Gala apples (about 6 pounds), peeled, cored, and quartered
- 1 cup apple cider
- 1/4 cup sugar, plus more to taste
- 1 whole cinnamon stick
- 1 teaspoon ground ginger, plus more to taste
- 1/2 teaspoon ground nutmeg, plus more to taste
- 2 tablespoons freshly squeezed lemon juice
- 1 vanilla bean, split lengthwise and scraped

Combine all ingredients in a large, wide, heavy-bottom saucepan over medium heat. Cover; cook, stirring occasionally with a wooden spoon to prevent scorching, until apples have broken down and are saucy, 50 to 60 minutes. Discard cinnamon stick and vanilla pod. Mash any large pieces of apple with the spoon. Add more sugar and spices, as desired. Remove from heat; let cool.

POTATO ROSTI

SERVES 8 TO 10

Rösti *is a Swiss term meaning "crisp and golden." Potato rösti is usually fried in a skillet; we bake it for a leaner version.*

- 1/4 cup extra-virgin olive oil, plus more for baking sheet
- 2 large onions, grated on the large holes of a box grater
- 5 pounds Yukon gold (about 10 medium) or russet potatoes
- 8 ounces freshly grated Swiss cheese (about 2 cups)
- 1 tablespoon coarse salt
- 3/4 teaspoon freshly ground pepper

1. Preheat oven to 375°F, with rack in lower third. Brush a 16 1/2-by-11 1/2-inch rimmed baking sheet generously with oil.

2. Place onions in a large bowl. Peel potatoes, and grate on the large holes of a box grater, adding them to the bowl and stirring into onions as you work (to prevent discoloration). Squeeze handfuls of grated potato and onion to release excess water, and transfer to another bowl. Add cheese, salt, pepper, and oil; toss to combine.

3. Sprinkle potato mixture over prepared baking sheet, and press lightly to form an even layer. Bake until golden, about 1 hour. Remove from oven, and cut into squares. Serve immediately.

GREEN BEANS WITH SPAETZLE

SERVES 8 TO 10

Spaetzle—a German dish of tiny noodles—is often made by forcing dough through the large holes of a colander into boiling water; we like to use a potato ricer.

- 2 1/2 cups all-purpose flour
- 1/2 teaspoon freshly grated nutmeg
- 1/4 cup minced fresh flat-leaf parsley leaves, plus more for garnish
- Coarse salt and freshly ground pepper
- 2/3 cup milk
- 5 large eggs
- 7 tablespoons extra-virgin olive oil
- 2 pounds green beans, trimmed and cut into 1 1/2-inch pieces

1. Whisk together flour, nutmeg, and parsley in a large bowl; season with salt and pepper. In another bowl, whisk together the milk, eggs, and 5 tablespoons oil until combined. Whisk milk mixture into flour mixture until smooth.

2. In a large stockpot, bring 6 quarts water to a boil; add salt. Working in batches, pass batter through a potato ricer, fitted with a 1/6-inch-hole attachment, into the boiling water. Cook until noodles float to the top, about 30 seconds. Using a slotted spoon, transfer noodles to a colander to drain. Repeat until all batter is used.

3. Heat remaining 2 tablespoons oil in a large nonstick skillet over medium-high heat. Add green beans, and sauté until just tender and bright green. Add spaetzle, season with salt and pepper, and cook until heated through. Serve immediately, garnished with parsley.

ORANGE SPIRAL ROLLS

MAKES 3 DOZEN

- 1 1/4 cups warm water
- 2 envelopes active dry yeast (each 1/4 ounce)
- 1/2 cup solid vegetable shortening, melted
- 1 cup sugar
- 2 teaspoons salt
- 3 large eggs
- Finely grated zest of 2 oranges, plus juice of 1 orange (about 1/3 cup)
- 5 cups all-purpose flour, plus more for work surface
- Vegetable oil, for bowl
- Cooking spray
- 6 tablespoons unsalted butter, melted

1. Place warm water in the bowl of an electric mixer, and sprinkle with yeast. Let stand until foamy, about 5 minutes.

2. Add shortening, 1/2 cup sugar, and salt to yeast mixture. Attach bowl to mixer fitted with the paddle attachment, and beat until smooth and combined. Add eggs and half the orange zest; beat until combined.

3. With the mixer on low speed, add flour, 1/2 cup at a time, beating until incorporated after each addition. Transfer to a floured work surface, and knead slightly to form a ball. Place in an oiled bowl, cover loosely with plastic wrap, and let rise in a warm place until doubled in bulk, about 1 hour.

4. Punch down dough with your hands, and cover again with plastic wrap. Refrigerate overnight. About 4 hours before proceeding with recipe, remove dough from refrigerator, and let stand at room temperature.

5. Coat three 12-cup muffin tins with cooking spray. In a medium bowl, whisk together remaining 1/2 cup sugar and orange zest with the orange juice and butter.

6. Divide dough into three equal pieces, and cover with plastic wrap or a damp kitchen towel. On a lightly floured work surface, roll out 1 piece into an 8-by-14-inch rectangle (let rest a few minutes if dough resists). Brush top of dough with some orange mixture; starting at one long side, roll into a tight cylinder. Cut crosswise into 12 slices, about 1 inch thick. Repeat with remaining 2 pieces of dough. Place slices in prepared muffin tins. Cover loosely with plastic wrap coated with cooking spray. Let dough rise until it fills cups, about 45 minutes.

7. Meanwhile, preheat oven to 375°F. Remove plastic wrap, and gently brush tops of rolls with remaining orange mixture. Bake until rolls are golden brown, 10 to 12 minutes. Remove from oven, and let cool slightly before serving.

MILE-HIGH APPLE PIE

MAKES ONE 9-INCH PIE

Resist the urge to cut this pie before it has cooled completely so the juices have time to thicken. This pie tastes even better the day after it has been baked.

- Deep-Dish Pâte Brisée (recipe follows)
- 6 tablespoons all-purpose flour, plus more for work surface
- 5 1/2 pounds firm, tart apples, such as Empire or Granny Smith
- Juice of 2 lemons
- 1 cup granulated sugar
- 2 teaspoons ground cinnamon
- 3 tablespoons chilled unsalted butter, cut into small pieces
- 1 large egg yolk
- Sanding sugar, for sprinkling

1. On a lightly floured work surface, roll out 1 piece of dough to an 11-inch round, about 1/8 inch thick, dusting work surface with flour as needed to prevent sticking. Brush off excess flour with a dry pastry brush. Roll dough around rolling pin, and lift it over a deep-dish 9-inch pie pan. Fit dough into pan, gently pressing it into bottom and up sides. Trim dough so that it hangs over pie plate by about 1/4 inch. Roll out another piece of dough to an 11-inch round. Transfer dough round to a parchment-lined baking sheet, and refrigerate along with pie shell, 30 minutes.

2. Preheat oven to 450°F. Peel and core apples, and cut into 1/4-inch-thick slices. As you cut, place slices in a large bowl, and sprinkle with lemon juice (to prevent discoloration). In a small bowl, combine flour, granulated sugar, and cinnamon; toss with apple slices.

3. Remove dough from refrigerator. Place apples in prepared pan, mounding them in a tall pile. Dot apples with butter. In a small dish, whisk egg yolk with 2 tablespoons water; brush glaze on edge of pie shell. Center and place other dough round over apples. Tuck edges of top dough under bottom dough, on top of rim of pan; gently press along edge to seal, and crimp as desired.

4. Roll out remaining piece of dough, if desired, and cut out apple or leaf shapes with cookie cutters. Brush bottoms with glaze, and press to adhere to top edge of shell.

5. Using a sharp paring knife, cut several vents in top dough to let steam escape. Brush surface with egg glaze; sprinkle with sanding sugar. Bake until golden brown on top, about 15 minutes. Reduce oven temperature to 350°F; continue baking until crust is golden brown and juices are bubbling, 45 to 50 minutes. Remove from oven; let cool completely before serving.

DEEP-DISH PATE BRISEE

MAKES ENOUGH FOR ONE 9-INCH DOUBLE-CRUST DEEP-DISH PIE

This dough can be frozen, wrapped well in plastic, for up to one month. Defrost completely in the refrigerator before using.

- 3 3/4 cups all-purpose flour
- 1 1/2 teaspoons salt
- 1 1/2 teaspoons sugar
- 1 1/2 cups (3 sticks) chilled unsalted butter, cut into small pieces
- 1/2 to 3/4 cup ice water

1. In a food processor, pulse together flour, salt, and sugar to combine. Add butter, and process until mixture resembles coarse meal, about 10 seconds. With machine running, add 1/2 cup ice water in a slow, steady stream through the feed tube, just until dough holds together. Test dough by pinching a small amount; if it is still crumbly, add up to 1/4 cup more ice water, a little at a time. Do not process more than 30 seconds.

2. Turn out dough onto a clean work surface, and divide into 3 equal pieces. Place each piece on plastic wrap, and flatten into a disk; wrap tightly. Refrigerate at least 1 hour before using.

CHOCOLATE- AND BUTTERSCOTCH-CHIP COOKIES

MAKES ABOUT 4 DOZEN

- 2 cups all-purpose flour
- 1 teaspoon baking soda
- 1/4 teaspoon salt
- 1 1/4 cups (2 1/2 sticks) unsalted butter, room temperature
- 1 cup granulated sugar
- 3/4 cup packed dark-brown sugar
- 2 large eggs
- 1 teaspoon pure vanilla extract
- 1 cup butterscotch chips
- 1 cup semisweet chocolate chips

1. Preheat oven to 350°F. Line two large baking sheets with parchment paper, and set aside. In a medium bowl, whisk together flour, baking soda, and salt; set aside. In the bowl of an electric mixer fitted with the paddle attachment, cream butter and sugars until light and fluffy, about 3 minutes. Beat in eggs and vanilla until well combined. Add flour mixture, and beat until just incorporated. Stir in both chips.

2. Working in batches, drop batter by the tablespoon onto prepared baking sheets, 2 inches apart. Bake until golden brown, rotating sheets halfway through, about 12 minutes. Transfer to a wire rack; let cool on baking sheets 1 minute before transferring cookies to rack.

BRATSELIES

MAKES ABOUT 6 DOZEN

This is a family recipe passed down from Vera Carlson, great aunt of Brooke Hellewell Reynolds, who is a senior art director at Martha Stewart Kids. *We used a special iron, which makes four cookies at a time, but you can also use a pizzelle iron. These wafer-thin cookies can be stored in an airtight container in the refrigerator for up to two weeks.*

- 7 to 9 cups all-purpose flour, sifted
- 1/4 teaspoon salt
- 1 tablespoon ground cinnamon
- 1 cup (2 sticks) unsalted butter, room temperature
- 1 1/2 cups sugar
- Finely grated zest of 1 lemon (optional)
- 1 tablespoon pure vanilla extract
- 1 tablespoon pure lemon extract
- 2 large eggs, lightly beaten, room temperature
- 1 cup heavy cream, room temperature
- Cooking spray

1. In a medium bowl, whisk together 3 cups flour, salt, and cinnamon; set aside. In the bowl of an electric mixer fitted with the paddle attachment, cream butter and sugar until light and fluffy. Add lemon zest, if using, and extracts; beat until combined. Add eggs, and beat until combined.

2. In a separate bowl, whisk cream until just slightly thickened. Add to butter mixture, then add flour mixture; beat until combined. Add 4 more cups flour, 1 cup at a time, beating until incorporated after each addition, until dough is soft enough to handle but still slightly sticky. If necessary, add up to 2 more cups flour, 1 cup at a time. Pinch off 1/2-teaspoon pieces of dough, and roll into balls; place on baking sheets.

3. Coat iron with cooking spray, and heat. Place 1 ball of dough in each grid, and press handle down tightly. Cook until golden, 20 to 25 seconds. Using a spatula, transfer cookies to a cutting board; cut into 4 wedges with a sharp knife. Let cool completely. Store, refrigerated, in an airtight container up to 2 weeks.

ALMOND SHORTBREAD COOKIES

MAKES ABOUT 3 DOZEN

- 1 cup all-purpose flour
- 1 cup cornstarch
- 3/4 teaspoon ground cardamom
- 1 teaspoon freshly ground white pepper
- 1/2 teaspoon salt
- 1 cup (2 sticks) unsalted butter, room temperature
- 2 1/2 cups confectioners' sugar, sifted
- 1 teaspoon pure almond extract
- 1 large egg white
- 72 whole blanched almonds (about 4 ounces)

1. Line two large baking sheets with parchment paper; set aside. In a medium bowl, whisk together flour, cornstarch, cardamom, pepper, and salt; set mixture aside.

2. In the bowl of an electric mixer fitted with the paddle attachment, cream butter and 1 cup confectioners' sugar until light and fluffy. Add almond extract, and beat to combine. With mixer on low speed, gradually add flour mixture until a dough forms, scraping down sides of bowl as needed.

3. Pinch off tablespoons of dough, and roll into 1 1/2-inch balls. Place on prepared baking sheets, 2 inches apart. Flatten each ball slightly with your fingertips. Cover with plastic wrap, and chill 30 minutes.

4. Preheat oven to 325°F. Whisk egg white in a small bowl. Add almonds; toss to coat. Remove dough from refrigerator; press 2 almonds on top of each ball of dough.

5. Bake until slightly golden, about 18 minutes. Remove from oven, and immediately transfer cookies to a wire rack.

6. Place remaining 1 1/2 cups confectioners' sugar in a medium bowl. While cookies are warm, roll them in sugar, reserving remaining sugar. Return cookies to baking sheets, and let cool 15 minutes more; roll again in sugar. Store cookies in an airtight container at room temperature up to 1 week.

CHOCOLATE FUDGE

MAKES ABOUT 3 POUNDS

This fudge is even better the day after it is made. You will need to pull the fudge on a clean work surface; we like to use a marble slab or a lightly buttered baking sheet.

- 4½ cups sugar
- ½ cup Dutch-process cocoa powder
- 1½ cups heavy cream
- ½ cup (1 stick) unsalted butter, plus more for fingertips
- 3 tablespoons light corn syrup
- 1½ teaspoons pure vanilla extract
- 1½ cups chopped nuts, such as pecans or almonds (optional)

1. Line an 8-inch square baking pan with waxed paper; set aside. In a medium heavy saucepan, stir together sugar and cocoa. Add cream, butter, and corn syrup; cook over medium-high heat, stirring constantly, just until mixture begins to bubble around the edges, about 5 minutes. Continue cooking, without stirring, until mixture reaches the soft-ball stage on a candy thermometer (238°F to 240°F), 12 to 15 minutes, washing down sides of pan with a pastry brush dipped in water to prevent crystals from forming. Immediately remove from heat; let cool in pan until temperature is 160°F, about 40 minutes. Do not stir until the mixture has cooled, because stirring will cause crystals to form.

2. When temperature reaches 160°F, quickly pour fudge onto clean work surface, using a rubber spatula to gently empty pan (hold pan very close to surface to prevent splattering). Spoon vanilla extract over fudge, and let cool until fudge is almost at room temperature, about 15 minutes more.

3. Using a long offset spatula, begin pulling fudge in a figure-eight motion, moving from the bottom right up and over to the top left, around to the right, and back down to the bottom left. Repeat, from bottom left, up and over to the top right and back down, pushing fudge onto itself. Continue this process until you see a sudden change in appearance, from glossy to flat, 12 to 15 minutes. Sprinkle with nuts, if desired, and stir to combine.

4. Spread fudge into prepared pan, and flatten with lightly buttered fingertips. Cover with waxed paper, and let stand until set, at least 4 hours or overnight. To prevent fudge from drying out, cut it into squares just before serving.

PEANUT BRITTLE

MAKES ONE 9-BY-13-INCH SQUARE

Although brittle with peanuts is the most common variety, you can instead use other whole nuts, such as cashews, hazelnuts, almonds, or pecans, as well as toasted pumpkin seeds.

- Unsalted butter, room temperature, for baking sheet
- 1½ cups sugar
- ½ cup light corn syrup
- Pinch of salt
- 2½ cups dry-roasted peanuts
- 1 teaspoon pure vanilla extract
- 1 teaspoon baking soda
- Vegetable oil, for spatula

1. Brush a 9-by-13-inch rimmed baking sheet with butter; set aside. Combine sugar, corn syrup, salt, and ¾ cup water in a medium saucepan. Bring to a boil over medium-high heat, stirring until sugar has dissolved. Cook, swirling pan occasionally (do not stir), until mixture reaches the soft-ball stage on a candy thermometer (238°F to 240°F); wash down sides of pan with a pastry brush dipped in water to prevent crystals from forming. Stir in nuts; continue cooking, stirring frequently with a wooden spoon to prevent nuts from burning, until mixture is light amber in color.

2. Remove from heat. Carefully stir in vanilla and baking soda (the mixture will foam up in the pan). Pour onto prepared baking sheet, and quickly spread into a ½-inch-thick layer with an oiled metal spatula. Let cool completely.

3. Break brittle into large pieces; store in an airtight container at room temperature for up to 1 month.

GINGERBREAD DOUGH FOR HOUSES

MAKES 3 POUNDS OF DOUGH

- 4½ cups flour, plus more as needed
- 3 teaspoons ground ginger
- 2 teaspoons ground cinnamon
- 1 teaspoon ground cloves
- 1 teaspoon ground nutmeg
- 1 teaspoon baking soda
- 1 teaspoon salt
- ½ teaspoon freshly ground pepper
- 1 cup solid vegetable shortening
- 1 cup sugar
- 1 cup molasses

1. Into a large bowl, sift together flour, spices, baking soda, salt, and pepper; set aside. In a large saucepan, melt shortening over medium-high heat, about 4 minutes. Whisk in sugar and molasses until combined. Remove from heat; stir in flour mixture until just combined and still crumbly. If dough is still sticky, add a bit more flour.

2. Turn out dough onto a large piece of plastic wrap, and wrap to enclose completely; let cool slightly, 10 to 15 minutes.

3. Preheat oven to 325°F, and line a large baking sheet with a Silpat baking mat. While dough is still slightly warm, roll out gently but firmly to a ⅜-inch thickness on baking mat. Following directions on page 27, cut out house facade, props, and shutters.

4. Bake 30 minutes, rotating sheet halfway through. Transfer baking sheet to a wire rack, and allow to cool completely before decorating.

ROYAL ICING

MAKES ABOUT 5 CUPS

Royal icing can be made several days in advance. Make sure to beat it well with a rubber spatula before using.

- 2 pounds confectioners' sugar
- ½ cup plus 2 tablespoons meringue powder
- Gel paste food colors (optional)

1. Combine all ingredients with a scant 1 cup water in the bowl of an electric mixer fitted with the paddle attachment; mix on low speed until icing becomes fluffy but dense, 7 to 8 minutes. Use immediately, or transfer to an airtight container (royal icing hardens quickly when exposed to air). Stir well with spatula before using.

2. Divide icing among three bowls. Use one bowl for attaching props and shutters (icing should be quite thick). Thin icing in remaining two bowls as needed by stirring in additional water, 1 teaspoon at a time: For piping designs, add just enough water so icing is no longer stiff; for floodwork, add water until icing is the consistency of honey (test by lifting spoon and letting icing drip back into bowl; ribbon of icing on surface should remain for 5 to 7 seconds).

3. To color icing, dip the tip of a toothpick into color, and gradually mix into icing until mixture reaches desired color.

SUGAR SYRUP

MAKES ABOUT 2 CUPS

The sugar syrup is very hot, so as you work with it, keep children at a safe distance.

- 1 cup sugar
- ½ cup light corn syrup

1. Combine ingredients and 1 cup water in a small saucepan over medium-high heat. Bring to a boil, periodically wiping down sides of pan with a pastry brush dipped in water to prevent crystals from forming.

2. Boil syrup until light yellow in color and temperature reaches 300°F on a candy thermometer (just under hard-crack stage). Remove saucepan from stove, and pour syrup into a large heatproof measuring cup, (this makes it safer and easier to pour the hot syrup, and it stops the cooking process). Use immediately, following directions on page 29 to make windows for the gingerbread house.

TREE-TRIMMING DESSERT PARTY

APPLE-ROSEMARY TART

MAKES ONE 9-INCH TART

Serve this lattice-top tart with freshly whipped cream or vanilla ice cream.

- All-purpose flour, for work surface
- Walnut Pâte Brisée (recipe follows)
- 4 Rome Beauty or other baking apples
- Juice of 1 lemon
- 2 sprigs rosemary, leaves picked, plus more sprigs for garnish
- ¼ cup sugar
- 2 teaspoons cornstarch
- 2 tablespoons unsalted butter, chilled and cut into small pieces
- Glazed Walnut Halves (recipe follows)

1. On a lightly floured work surface, roll out one disk of dough to an 11-inch circle, about ⅛ inch thick. Roll dough around rolling pin, and unroll over a 9-inch fluted tart pan with a removable bottom. Using your fingers, gently press dough into bottom and sides of pan; roll pin over top to trim excess flush with edge of pan. Refrigerate tart shell 30 minutes.

2. Meanwhile, roll out remaining disk of dough to an ⅛-inch thickness. Using a fluted pastry wheel, cut into ten ¾-by-12-inch strips. Transfer strips to a parchment-lined baking sheet, and chill 30 minutes.

3. Peel, core, and cut each apple into 16 wedges. In a medium bowl, toss wedges with lemon juice and rosemary leaves. In a small bowl, combine sugar and cornstarch. Sprinkle mixture over apples; toss to coat.

4. Preheat oven to 400°F. Line tart shell with parchment paper, leaving about 2 inches of overhang; fill with pie weights or dried beans. Bake until crust starts to take on color, about 15 minutes. Remove parchment and weights. Reduce oven temperature to 350°F; continue baking until crust is lightly browned and firm to the touch, about 7 more minutes.

5. Fill crust with apple mixture, and dot with butter. Using chilled strips of dough, weave a lattice pattern over the top; trim ends flush with edge of pan, and press into bottom crust. Bake until lattice crust is lightly browned and apples are tender, about 1 hour. Remove from oven; transfer to a wire rack to cool slightly. Decorate tart with glazed walnuts, and garnish serving piece with rosemary sprigs. Serve warm.

WALNUT PATE BRISEE

MAKES ONE 9-INCH LATTICE-TOP TART

Dough can be frozen for up to one month; thaw overnight in the refrigerator before using.

- 2 cups all-purpose flour
- 1 teaspoon salt
- 1 teaspoon sugar
- ½ cup walnut pieces (about 2 ounces)
- ¾ cups (1½ sticks) chilled unsalted butter, cut into pieces
- ¼ to ½ cup ice water

1. In a food processor, pulse flour, salt, sugar, and walnuts until nuts are coarsely chopped, about 10 seconds. Add butter; pulse until mixture forms pea-size clumps.

2. With machine running, add ¼ cup ice water in a slow, steady stream through the feed tube, just until dough starts to come together. Test dough by pinching a small amount; if it is still crumbly, add up to ¼ cup more ice water, a little at a time. Do not process more than 30 seconds.

3. Turn out dough onto a clean work surface, and divide in half. Place each piece on plastic wrap, and flatten into a disk; wrap tightly. Refrigerate at least 1 hour before using.

GLAZED WALNUT HALVES

MAKES ENOUGH FOR ONE 9-INCH TART

- 9 walnut halves
- 2 tablespoons honey

Preheat oven to 400°F. Line a small baking sheet with parchment paper. In a small bowl, toss together walnuts and honey. Place coated walnuts on prepared baking sheet; bake until glazed and shiny, 8 to 9 minutes. Transfer sheet to a wire rack to cool. Store in an airtight container at room temperature up to 2 days.

APRICOT TEA CAKES

MAKES 1 DOZEN

Unsalted butter, for cake rings
All-purpose flour, for cake rings
1¾ cups yellow cornmeal
1 cup milk
1 cup sugar
¼ teaspoon salt
Grated zest and juice of 1 orange
4 large eggs, separated
3 tablespoons olive oil
24 apricot halves in syrup (two 8½-ounce cans), drained and dried on paper towels
12 whole unblanched almonds
½ cup honey

1. Preheat oven to 375°F. Line a rimmed baking sheet with parchment paper. Butter and flour twelve 3-by-1½-inch cake rings; place on prepared baking sheet. Place cornmeal in a large bowl; set aside.
2. In a small saucepan, bring milk, sugar, salt, and orange zest to a boil over medium-high heat, stirring to dissolve sugar. Slowly pour hot milk mixture over cornmeal, mixing with a fork. Cover with plastic wrap, and let stand in a warm place 30 minutes.
3. Add orange juice to cornmeal mixture, then add egg yolks one at a time, stirring well after each addition. Stir in oil.
4. In a medium bowl, beat egg whites until stiff and shiny. Fold into cornmeal mixture.
5. Place one apricot half, cut side up, in center of each cake ring. Pour ½ cup batter into each ring. Bake 5 minutes, and remove from oven. Reduce oven heat to 325°F. Place another apricot half, cut side up, in center of each cake, and place an almond in center of each apricot. Return to oven, and bake until tops are golden brown, about 25 minutes.
6. Transfer baking sheet to a wire rack, and let cool 5 minutes. Remove rings, and let cool completely. Before serving, drizzle cakes evenly with honey.

ORANGE-CORNMEAL COOKIES

MAKES ABOUT 3 DOZEN

1 cup (2 sticks) unsalted butter, room temperature
1¼ cups sugar
Grated zest of 2 oranges
1 teaspoon pure vanilla extract
4 large whole eggs
2 large egg yolks
3 cups all-purpose flour, sifted
2 cups yellow cornmeal

1. Preheat oven to 375°F, with racks in center and lower third. Line two baking sheets with parchment paper, and set aside. In the bowl of an electric mixer fitted with the paddle attachment, cream butter, sugar, orange zest, and vanilla until light and fluffy. Add eggs and yolks one at a time, beating until combined after each addition. Add flour and cornmeal, and beat on low speed until just combined.
2. Spoon a third of the batter into a pastry bag fitted with a large star tip (Ateco #825). Pipe batter onto prepared baking sheets in S shapes, each about 3 inches long and 1½ inches apart.
3. Bake until golden brown on bottoms and around edges, rotating sheets halfway through, about 22 minutes. Transfer to a wire rack; let cool on baking sheets 5 minutes, then transfer to rack to cool completely. Store cookies in an airtight container at room temperature up to 3 days.

CHESTNUT TRUFFLES

MAKES ABOUT 2 DOZEN

Uncoated truffles can be stored in an airtight container in the refrigerator for up to five days; roll them in sugar or cocoa just before serving.

½ cup heavy cream
8 ounces semisweet chocolate, finely chopped
2 tablespoons dark corn syrup
12 chestnuts packed in syrup, drained, patted dry, and coarsely chopped
¼ cup confectioners' sugar
¼ cup unsweetened cocoa powder

1. Bring cream to a simmer in a small saucepan over medium heat; remove from heat. Add chocolate and corn syrup, stirring until chocolate is melted. Fold in chestnuts; transfer to a medium bowl, and refrigerate until set, about 1 hour.
2. Scoop out about 2 teaspoons chocolate mixture; using fingers, form into roughly shaped balls. Place on a parchment-lined baking sheet. Refrigerate until cold and firm, 15 to 30 minutes.
3. When ready to serve, roll some balls in confectioners' sugar for a white coating; roll the rest in cocoa for a brown coating. Coat completely.

POACHED PEARS WITH THREE SAUCES

SERVES 6

6 ripe but firm pears, such as Anjou, Bartlett, or Bosc, peeled
1 bottle (750 ml) dry white wine
1 cup sugar
2 vanilla beans, split lengthwise and scraped
2 whole cinnamon sticks
4 whole cloves
Peel from 1 orange
Peel from 1 lemon
2 whole pods star anise
2 dried bay leaves
Warm Chocolate Sauce, for serving (recipe follows)
Mascarpone Cream, for serving (recipe follows)

1. Place all ingredients except sauces in a large pot. Fill with just enough water to cover pears, and place a lid or plate small enough to fit inside pot on top of pears so they stay submerged. Bring water to a boil. Reduce heat to a simmer, and cook until pears are tender when pierced with the tip of a paring knife, 10 to 15 minutes. Remove from heat; let pears cool in liquid. (Pears and liquid can be refrigerated, covered, up to 1 day.)
2. Using a slotted spoon, transfer pears to an airtight container. Pour poaching liquid through a fine sieve set over a bowl; discard solids, and return liquid to saucepan. To make spiced syrup, cook over medium-high

heat until liquid is thick enough to coat the back of a spoon, about 1 hour. Set aside to cool.

3. When ready to serve, cut a very small slice off bottom of each pear so it stands upright. Arrange pears in a large bowl, and set out with small bowls of spiced syrup, chocolate sauce, and mascarpone cream so guests can choose among them.

WARM CHOCOLATE SAUCE

MAKES ABOUT 1¼ CUPS

- 6 ounces bittersweet chocolate, coarsely chopped
- ¾ cup plus 1 tablespoon heavy cream

Place chocolate in a small heatproof bowl. In a small saucepan, heat cream until steaming. Pour over chocolate, and let stand 5 minutes; stir until smooth. Keep warm over a pan of simmering water until ready to use.

MASCARPONE CREAM

MAKES ABOUT 2 CUPS

- 4 ounces mascarpone cheese
- 3 tablespoons sugar
- 1½ tablespoons dark rum
- ½ cup heavy cream, whipped

In a medium bowl, whisk together mascarpone, sugar, and rum. Gently fold in whipped cream. Refrigerate sauce, covered, up to 2 days.

DOBOS TORTE

SERVES 12

- 6 tablespoons unsalted butter, melted, plus more for baking sheets
- 1½ cups all-purpose flour, plus more for baking sheets
- 1 cup sugar
- 6 large eggs
- ¼ teaspoon salt
- ½ teaspoon pure vanilla extract
- ½ teaspoon pure almond extract
- Hazelnut Simple Syrup (recipe follows)
- Caramel Buttercream (recipe follows)
- Caramel, for garnish (recipe follows)

1. Preheat oven to 350°F, with rack in center. Butter two 12-by-17-inch rimmed baking sheets. Line with parchment paper. Butter parchment; sprinkle with flour, tapping out excess. Set aside.

2. In the heatproof bowl of an electric mixer set over a pan of simmering water, whisk together sugar, eggs, and salt until mixture is warm and sugar has dissolved, about 2 minutes.

3. Attach bowl to mixer fitted with the whisk attachment, and beat mixture on high speed until very thick and pale, 6 to 8 minutes. Gently transfer mixture to a large shallow bowl.

4. Sift in 1 cup flour, ½ cup at a time, folding gently after each addition. In a bowl, combine melted butter and extracts; add to egg mixture in a steady stream as you sift in remaining ½ cup flour; fold gently until just combined. Divide between prepared baking sheets; smooth tops with a spatula.

5. Bake until cakes are springy to the touch and light golden, 10 to 12 minutes. Transfer to a wire rack to cool completely. Invert cakes onto rack; remove parchment. Cut each cake into three 5¼-by-11¼-inch rectangles (you will use only 5; reserve or discard the remaining 1).

6. Lay a rectangle on a flat work surface. Using a pastry brush, soak with some simple syrup. Spread 1 cup buttercream evenly over top. Place another rectangle on top; continue until you have 5 layers soaked with syrup and topped with buttercream. Spread remaining buttercream over sides of cake, smoothing edges to form a neat block. Refrigerate until firm, at least 30 minutes. To serve, sprinkle chopped caramel over top.

HAZELNUT SIMPLE SYRUP

MAKES ABOUT 1⅛ CUPS

- ½ cup sugar
- ½ cup hazelnut liqueur, such as Frangelico

In a small saucepan, bring sugar and ½ cup water to a boil, swirling to dissolve sugar. Remove from heat. Cover, and let mixture cool completely. Stir in liqueur. Use immediately, or refrigerate in an airtight container up to 2 weeks.

CARAMEL BUTTERCREAM

MAKES ABOUT 2 QUARTS

- 2¼ cups sugar
- ½ cup heavy cream
- 9 large egg whites
- 3 cups (6 sticks) unsalted butter, room temperature, cut into tablespoons
- 1½ teaspoons pure vanilla extract

1. In a heavy medium saucepan, bring 1¼ cups sugar and ½ cup water to a boil over medium-high heat, stirring until sugar dissolves; wash down sides of pan with a pastry brush dipped in water to prevent crystals from forming. Continue cooking, without stirring but gently swirling pan to color evenly, until caramel is dark amber. Remove from heat; carefully pour in heavy cream (it will spatter), stirring with a wooden spoon until smooth. Let cool.

2. In the heatproof bowl of an electric mixer set over a pan of simmering water, gently whisk together egg whites and remaining cup sugar until warm to the touch and sugar has dissolved, about 3 minutes.

3. Attach bowl to mixer fitted with the whisk attachment; beat on medium speed until mixture is fluffy and cooled, about 10 minutes. Increase speed to high; whisk until stiff peaks form. Reduce speed to medium-low; add butter, a few tablespoons at a time, beating well after each addition. Beat in vanilla.

4. Switch to the paddle attachment. Add caramel mixture; beat on lowest speed until smooth, 3 to 5 minutes. Buttercream can be refrigerated in an airtight container up to 3 days. Before using, bring to room temperature; beat on lowest speed until smooth.

CARAMEL

MAKES ABOUT 1 CUP

Unsalted butter, for baking sheet
1/2 cup sugar

1. Butter a rimmed baking sheet. Bring sugar and 3 tablespoons water to a boil in a small, heavy saucepan, stirring until sugar dissolves; wash down sides of pan with a wet pastry brush to prevent crystals from forming. Continue cooking, without stirring but gently swirling pan to color evenly, until caramel is dark amber.
2. Immediately pour caramel onto prepared baking sheet. Let sit until hardened and completely cool; then coarsely chop. Store in an airtight container at room temperature up to 1 day.

A HOLIDAY BUFFET *of* SOUTHWESTERN FAVORITES

GUACAMOLE

SERVES 12 TO 18

Serve this dip with tortilla chips.

6 large ripe Hass avocados
4 scallions, trimmed and thinly sliced
3 tablespoons finely chopped fresh cilantro
2 tablespoons freshly squeezed lime juice
1/2 teaspoon ground cumin
Pinch of cayenne pepper
Coarse salt and freshly ground pepper

Halve avocados, and remove pits. Scoop out flesh into a medium bowl; mash with a potato masher, leaving some chunks for texture. Stir in scallions, cilantro, lime juice, cumin, and cayenne. Season with salt and pepper, and serve.

SPICE-RUBBED ROASTED RACK OF VENISON

SERVES 8

This recipe can easily be doubled.

2 tablespoons cumin seeds
2 tablespoons coriander seeds
1 tablespoon whole black peppercorns
1 tablespoon whole green peppercorns
1 tablespoon whole white peppercorns
4 shallots, minced
4 garlic cloves, minced
1/4 cup coarse salt
1/4 cup packed dark-brown sugar
1 rack of venison (8 chops; about 2 3/4 pounds)
1 tablespoon vegetable oil
Four-Onion and Jalapeño Confit (recipe follows), for serving

1. In a food processor, pulse seeds and peppercorns until coarsely ground, about 1 minute. Add shallots, garlic, salt, and sugar; process to a thick paste. Rinse venison, and pat dry. Rub a thin layer of paste all over meat. Wrap with plastic; chill at least 4 hours or overnight.
2. Preheat oven to 400°F. Rub off excess paste from venison. In an ovenproof skillet large enough to hold meat, heat oil over medium-high heat until just starting to smoke. Sear meat until browned, about 2 minutes per side. Transfer skillet to oven; cook to desired doneness, 15 to 18 minutes for medium-rare. Remove from oven; let rest 5 minutes before slicing. Serve with confit.

FOUR-ONION AND JALAPEÑO CONFIT

MAKES ABOUT 3 CUPS

This recipe can easily be doubled.

4 tablespoons unsalted butter
2 red onions, cut into 1/4-inch slices
2 sweet yellow onions, cut into 1/4-inch slices
4 large shallots, cut into 1/4-inch rings
10 garlic cloves, halved lengthwise
1 bunch scallions, trimmed and cut into 2-inch pieces
5 large jalapeño chiles, ribs and seeds removed, cut into 1/4-inch-wide strips
3/4 cup golden raisins
1/4 cup packed light-brown sugar
1/2 cup cider vinegar

1. Melt butter in a large saucepan over medium heat. Add onions, shallots, and garlic; cook, stirring occasionally, until vegetables begin to soften, about 8 minutes. Add remaining ingredients along with 1 1/2 cups water. Simmer, covered, until very tender, about 1 hour.
2. Uncover; simmer until thick and most liquid has evaporated, about 1 1/2 hours. Serve warm, or refrigerate in an airtight container up to 1 week.

TAMALES

Five tamale recipes follow, many of which were created with the help of Rick Bayless, author of several books on authentic Mexican cooking and chef-owner of Chicago's Frontera Grill and Topolobampo. Pick your favorites, making one or a few recipes, depending on the number of guests at your party. We used a bamboo steamer to cook the tamales, but you can use a metal steamer basket or a tamalera *instead (see "Tamales, A Christmas Tradition," page 51). Tamales are best right out of the steamer, but leftovers can be refrigerated, wrapped in plastic, for several days. To reheat, steam for twenty minutes. You can also freeze them for up to one month; without thawing, steam for thirty minutes to reheat.*

CHILE-CHEESE TAMALES

MAKES 16

4 ounces dried corn husks
3 cups fresh corn kernels (4 to 5 ears)
1/2 cup fresh pork lard or solid vegetable shortening (4 ounces)
2 cups coarsely ground fresh masa (1 pound) or 1 3/4 cups masa harina, mixed with 1 cup plus 2 tablespoons hot water and cooled to room temperature
2 tablespoons sugar
1 1/2 teaspoons salt
1 1/2 teaspoons baking powder
2 poblano chiles, roasted, seeds and ribs removed, cut into 1/4-inch strips
2 cups grated Monterey Jack cheese

1. Prepare corn husks: Place husks in a deep saucepan. Cover with water, and bring to a boil over high heat. Remove from heat; set a small plate on top of husks to keep them submerged. Let soak 1 hour.

2. Prepare batter: Process 2 cups corn kernels in a food processor until mixture is a coarse purée. Add lard, and pulse 5 or 6 times. Add masa mixture, sugar, salt, and baking powder. Process until mixture is light and fluffy, scraping down side of bowl once or twice, about 1 minute. The batter should be soft but hold its shape in a spoon. Transfer to a medium bowl; stir in remaining cup corn. Chill, covered, at least 1 hour.

3. Assemble tamales: Remove husks from water; reserve small husks to line steamer basket and cover tamales. Unroll 1 large piece; tear lengthwise along grain to make 1/4-inch-wide strips (you'll need 2 per tamale, for a total of 32 strips; if strips aren't long enough, tie 2 together). Remove another large piece; pat dry. Place on a clean work surface, pointed end away from you. Place 1/4 cup batter in middle of husk. Spread into a 4-inch square, leaving a 1 1/2-inch border on pointed end and a 1-inch border on other edges. Place some chile strips down center; sprinkle with 2 tablespoons cheese. Pick up sides of husk so batter encases filling; bring sides together to form a cylinder. Fold pointed end under; tie loosely with a husk strip. Fold flat end under, and tie with another strip. Repeat with remaining husks, batter, chiles, and cheese to assemble 16 tamales.

4. Steam tamales: Fill a wok or large skillet with 2 inches of water. Line bottom of a bamboo steamer basket with reserved corn husks; set basket in pan. Lay assembled tamales in basket; cover, and steam over high heat. When steam begins to release, reduce heat to medium. Continue steaming 1 hour 15 minutes, adding more water as necessary. To check for doneness, unwrap a tamale; dough should separate easily from wrapper and feel soft. If dough sticks to wrapper, rewrap, and steam 15 to 20 minutes more. Remove from heat; let stand at least 15 minutes and up to 1 hour before serving.

OAXACAN BLACK-BEAN TAMALES

MAKES 14

- 4 ounces dried corn husks
- 2/3 cup dried black beans, picked over
- 2 fresh or dried avocado leaves
- 2 tablespoons fresh pork lard or bacon drippings
- 1 small onion, cut into medium dice
- Coarse salt
- Classic Tamale Batter (recipe follows)
- Chopped Tomato and Serrano Salsa (recipe follows)

1. Prepare corn husks: Place husks in a deep saucepan, and cover with water. Bring to a boil over high heat. Remove from heat; set a small plate on top of husks to keep them submerged. Soak 1 hour.

2. Prepare filling: In a small saucepan, combine black beans, avocado leaves, lard, onion, and 3 cups water. Bring to a boil over high heat, then reduce heat to medium-low. Simmer, partially covered, until beans are very tender, about 1 1/2 hours; add more water as necessary during cooking. Remove and discard avocado leaves. Generously season filling with salt; set aside to cool. Using a potato masher or a large spoon, coarsely mash filling until it holds together when scooped with a spoon.

3. Assemble tamales: Remove husks from water; reserve small husks to line steamer basket and cover tamales. Unroll 1 large piece; tear lengthwise along grain to make 1/4-inch-wide strips (you'll need 2 per tamale, for a total of 28 strips; if strips aren't long enough, tie 2 together). Remove another large piece; pat dry. Place on a clean work surface, pointed end away from you. Place 1/4 cup batter in middle of husk. Spread into a 4-inch square, leaving a 1 1/2-inch border on pointed end and a 1-inch border on other edges. Spoon 2 tablespoons black-bean filling down center. Pick up sides of husk so batter encases filling; bring sides together, forming a cylinder. Fold pointed end under; tie loosely with a husk strip. Fold flat end under, and tie with another strip. Repeat with remaining husks, batter, and filling to assemble 14 tamales.

4. Steam tamales: Fill a wok or large skillet with 2 inches of water. Line bottom of a bamboo steamer basket with reserved corn husks; set basket in pan. Lay assembled tamales in basket; cover, and steam over high heat. When steam begins to release, reduce heat to medium. Continue steaming 1 hour 15 minutes, adding more water as necessary. To check for doneness, unwrap a tamale; dough should separate easily from wrapper and feel soft. If dough sticks to wrapper, rewrap, and steam 15 to 20 minutes more. Remove from heat; let stand at least 15 minutes and up to 1 hour before serving with the salsa.

CLASSIC TAMALE BATTER

MAKES 3 3/4 CUPS

You can use chicken, beef, or vegetable stock in this recipe; choose one that best suits the tamale filling. If you cannot find freshly rendered pork lard, use solid vegetable shortening, not canned or packaged lard. The batter can be stored in an airtight container in the refrigerator for up to two days.

- 5 ounces fresh pork lard (2/3 cup), chilled
- 1 teaspoon baking powder
- 1 scant teaspoon salt
- 2 cups coarsely ground fresh masa (1 pound) or 1 3/4 cups masa harina, mixed with 1 cup plus 2 tablespoons hot water and cooled to room temperature
- 2/3 cup chicken, beef, or vegetable stock, preferably homemade

In the bowl of an electric mixer fitted with the paddle attachment, combine lard, baking powder, and salt. Beat until light and fluffy. Add 1 cup masa mixture and 1/3 cup stock; beat until thoroughly combined. Add remaining masa mixture and 1/3 cup stock; beat until light and fluffy, about 2 minutes. The batter should be soft but hold its shape in a spoon. (If using fresh masa, test the batter to determine if it is adequately fluffy: Drop 1 teaspoon batter into 1 cup cold water. If it floats to the surface, it is ready. If not, continue beating.) Refrigerate, covered, at least 1 hour.

CHOPPED TOMATO AND SERRANO SALSA

MAKES 2 CUPS

Although this salsa is at its best when made within about an hour of serving, it can be stored in an airtight container in the refrigerator for up to two days.

- 1 small white onion, finely diced
- 12 ounces plum tomatoes, finely diced
- 4 fresh serrano chiles, stems removed, finely chopped
- 12 large sprigs fresh cilantro, finely chopped
- 1 large garlic clove, minced
- 1½ teaspoons freshly squeezed lime juice
- Coarse salt

Place onion in a fine sieve, and rinse under cold running water. Shake sieve to remove any excess water. Transfer onion to a medium bowl, and add remaining ingredients. Stir to combine; let stand a few minutes so flavors meld.

BUTTERY FRESH CORN TAMALES

MAKES 14

- 4 ounces dried corn husks
- 2¾ cups fresh corn kernels (3 to 4 ears)
- ½ cup (1 stick) unsalted butter, cut into tablespoons
- 2 cups coarsely ground fresh masa (1 pound) or 1¾ cups masa harina, mixed with 1 cup plus 2 tablespoons hot water and cooled to room temperature
- 2 tablespoons sugar
- ½ teaspoon salt
- 1½ teaspoons baking powder
- 1 cup sour cream, for serving (optional)
- Chopped Tomato and Serrano Salsa (recipe above)

1. Prepare corn husks: Place husks in a deep saucepan, and cover with water. Bring to a boil over high heat. Remove from heat; set a small plate on top of husks to keep them submerged. Soak 1 hour.

2. Prepare batter: Process 2 cups corn kernels in a food processor until mixture is a coarse purée. Add butter, and pulse 5 or 6 times. Add masa mixture, sugar, salt, and baking powder. Process until mixture is light and fluffy, scraping down sides of bowl once or twice, about 1 minute. The batter should be soft but hold its shape in a spoon. Transfer to a medium bowl; stir in remaining ¾ cup corn. Chill, covered, at least 1 hour.

3. Assemble tamales: Remove husks from water; reserve small husks to line steamer basket and cover tamales. Unroll 1 large piece; tear lengthwise along grain to make ¼-inch-wide strips (you'll need 2 per tamale, for a total of 28 strips; if strips aren't long enough, tie 2 together). Remove another large piece; pat dry. Place on a clean work surface, pointed end away from you. Place ¼ cup batter in middle of husk. Spread into a 4-inch square, leaving a 1½-inch border on pointed end and a 1-inch border on other edges. Pick up sides of husk and bring together, forming a cylinder. Fold pointed end under; tie loosely with a husk strip. Fold flat end under, and tie with another strip. Repeat to assemble 14 tamales.

4. Steam tamales: Fill a wok or large skillet with 2 inches water. Line bottom of a bamboo steamer basket with reserved corn husks; set basket in pan. Lay assembled tamales in basket; cover, and steam over high heat. When steam begins to release, reduce heat to medium. Continue steaming 1 hour 15 minutes, adding more water as necessary. To check for doneness, unwrap a tamale; dough should separate easily from wrapper and feel soft. If dough sticks to wrapper, rewrap, and steam 15 to 20 minutes more. Remove from heat; let stand at least 15 minutes and up to 1 hour before serving with sour cream, if desired, and salsa.

RED-CHILE PORK TAMALES

MAKES 14

- 4 ounces dried corn husks
- 6 large dried New Mexico chiles, stems and seeds discarded, each chile torn into 4 pieces
- 2 garlic cloves, finely chopped
- ¼ teaspoon freshly ground pepper
- ⅛ teaspoon ground cumin
- 12 ounces lean boneless pork shoulder, cut into ½-inch cubes
- Coarse salt
- Classic Tamale Batter (page 117)
- Roasted-Tomatillo and Chipotle Salsa (recipe follows)

1. Prepare corn husks: Place husks in a deep saucepan, and cover with water. Bring to a boil over high heat. Remove from heat; set a small plate on top of husks to keep them submerged. Soak 1 hour.

2. Prepare filling: In a blender, purée chiles, garlic, pepper, cumin, and 1½ cups water until smooth. Strain mixture into a medium saucepan. Add pork and 1¾ cups water; season with salt. Cook over medium heat, stirring frequently, until liquid has reduced to the consistency of a thick sauce and meat is very tender, 50 to 60 minutes. Using a fork, break up the meat.

3. Place batter in a large bowl; stir in 3 tablespoons sauce until combined.

4. Assemble tamales: Remove husks from water; reserve small husks to line steamer basket and cover tamales. Unroll 1 large piece; tear lengthwise along grain to make ¼-inch-wide strips (you'll need 2 per tamale, for a total of 28 strips; if strips aren't long enough, tie 2 together). Remove another large piece; pat dry. Place on a clean work surface, pointed end away from you. Place ¼ cup batter in middle of husk. Spread into a 4-inch square, leaving a 1½-inch border on pointed end and a 1-inch border on other edges. Spoon 2 tablespoons pork filling down center. Pick up sides of husk so batter encases filling; bring sides together, forming a cylinder. Fold pointed end under; tie loosely with a husk strip. Fold flat end under; tie with another strip. Repeat with remaining husks, batter, and filling to assemble 14 tamales.

5. Steam tamales: Fill a wok or large skillet with 2 inches of water. Line bottom of a bamboo steamer basket with reserved corn husks; set basket in pan. Lay assembled tamales in basket; cover, and steam over high heat. When steam begins to release, reduce heat to medium. Continue steaming 1 hour 15 minutes, adding more water as necessary. To check for doneness, unwrap a tamale; the dough should separate easily from the wrapper and feel soft. If dough sticks to wrapper, rewrap, and steam 15 to 20 minutes more. Remove from heat, and let stand at least 15 minutes and up to 1 hour before serving with the salsa.

ROASTED-TOMATILLO AND CHIPOTLE SALSA

MAKES ABOUT 1¼ CUPS

This salsa tastes best the day it is made, but it can be refrigerated for up to one week in an airtight container.

- 3 large garlic cloves (unpeeled)
- 8 ounces tomatillos, husked and rinsed
- 5 canned chipotles in adobo, finely diced
- ½ teaspoon coarse salt
- ¼ teaspoon sugar

1. Heat broiler. Heat a small, heavy skillet over medium heat. Add garlic; cook, turning occasionally, until blackened in spots and soft, about 20 minutes. When cool enough to handle, peel garlic, and roughly chop.
2. Meanwhile, spread tomatillos on a baking sheet, and broil until blistered, blackened, and softened, about 10 minutes, turning once. Let cool completely.
3. Scrape tomatillos and juices into a food processor or blender. Add chopped garlic; pulse until a coarse purée forms. Stir in chiles, and add enough water (3 to 4 tablespoons) to make sauce spoonable. Stir in salt and sugar. Refrigerate in an airtight container up to 1 week.

VERACRUZANO PUDDING TAMALES WITH CHICKEN, CHIPOTLE, AND HERBS

MAKES 8

Fresh or frozen banana leaves are available at Mexican markets. If they are thick and not supple, roll them loosely, and steam over medium heat until they become pliable, about thirty minutes.

- 1 large boneless, skinless chicken breast
- Coarse salt
- 1 package fresh or frozen banana leaves
- 20 dried chipotle or morita chiles, stems removed
- 4 garlic cloves, unpeeled
- ½ teaspoon sugar
- 2 cups coarsely ground fresh masa (1 pound) or 1¾ cups masa harina, mixed with 1 cup plus 2 tablespoons hot water and cooled to room temperature
- 5 cups chicken stock, preferably homemade
- ½ cup fresh pork lard or solid vegetable shortening (4 ounces)
- 1 teaspoon table salt
- 3 large leaves fresh hoja santa or 24 sprigs fresh cilantro

1. Place the chicken breast in a medium saucepan; cover with salted water. Bring to a boil, then reduce heat to a simmer. Cook until chicken is opaque throughout, about 20 minutes. Remove from heat. When cool enough to handle, shred meat.
2. Using kitchen scissors, cut off brown, hard edges from banana leaves. From the trimmings, make sixteen ¼-inch-wide strips by cutting along the grain. Tie 2 strips together, forming 8 long strips; set leaves and strips aside. Reserve remaining pieces for lining steamer basket and covering tamales.
3. Heat a small, heavy skillet over medium heat. Add chiles; cook, stirring, until very fragrant and toasted in spots, 2 to 3 minutes. Transfer chiles to a heatproof bowl, and cover with 1½ cups hot water. Set a small plate on top of chiles to keep them submerged. Set aside to soak.
4. Meanwhile, add garlic to hot skillet; cook, turning, until darkened in spots and soft, about 20 minutes. Remove from heat. When cool enough to handle, peel garlic.
5. Drain chiles, reserving 1¼ cups soaking liquid. In a blender or food processor, purée chiles, reserved liquid, and garlic until smooth. Transfer purée to a small saucepan, and simmer over medium heat until mixture is the consistency of canned tomato sauce, 25 to 30 minutes. Stir in sugar, and season with coarse salt; set aside.
6. Prepare batter: Working in two batches, mix together masa and stock, and strain mixture through a medium sieve into a large saucepan. Bring to a boil over medium heat, whisking constantly, about 20 minutes. Whisk in lard until combined and mixture is thick enough to hold its shape when spooned, about 5 minutes. Add table salt; transfer to a bowl. Let cool completely.
7. Assemble tamales: Lay a banana leaf, shiny side down, on a clean work surface, and pat dry. Place ⅔ cup batter in the middle; spread batter toward the right side, forming a rough 3-by-6-inch rectangle. Place 1 tablespoon chipotle salsa, 2 tablespoons shredded chicken, and ¼ of a hoja santa leaf (or 3 sprigs cilantro) on the left side of the batter. Fold right third of leaf over, covering middle and encasing filling with batter. Fold uncovered section of leaf over the top, then fold both ends under. Tie a banana-leaf strip loosely around the middle. Repeat to form 8 tamales.
8. Steam tamales: Fill a wok or large skillet with 2 inches water. Line steamer basket with reserved pieces of banana leaves. Lay assembled tamales in basket, no more than 2 deep; cover, and steam over high heat. When steam begins to release, reduce heat to medium. Continue steaming 1 hour 15 minutes, adding more water as necessary. To check for doneness, unwrap a tamale; dough should separate easily from wrapper and feel soft. If dough sticks to wrapper, rewrap, and steam 15 to 20 minutes more. Remove from heat; let stand at least 15 minutes and up to 1 hour before serving with remaining salsa.

CHRISTMAS CORNBREAD

MAKES ONE 9-BY-13-INCH LOAF

- 1/4 cup plus 2 tablespoons solid vegetable shortening, plus more for pan
- 1 1/4 cups all-purpose flour
- 2 1/4 cups yellow cornmeal
- 2 teaspoons salt
- 1 1/2 teaspoons baking powder
- 3/4 teaspoon baking soda
- 3/4 teaspoon freshly ground pepper
- 3 large eggs
- 2 1/4 cups nonfat buttermilk
- 1 cup fresh corn kernels (from 1 ear)
- 2 jalapeño chiles, ribs and seeds discarded, minced
- 1 small red bell pepper, ribs and seeds discarded, cut into 1/4-inch dice
- 1 cup grated cheddar cheese

1. Preheat oven to 375°F. Coat a 9-by-13-inch baking pan with shortening. Whisk together flour, cornmeal, salt, baking powder, baking soda, and pepper in a bowl. Make a well in center; add eggs to well, and whisk into mixture. Add buttermilk, and whisk to combine (mixture will be thick). Stir in corn, chiles, bell pepper, and cheese.

2. Melt shortening in a small saucepan over medium heat. Pour hot shortening into corn mixture, and stir to combine. Spoon batter into prepared pan, spreading evenly. Bake until golden brown and pulling away from sides of pan, 20 to 30 minutes. Let stand in pan until cool to the touch; gently run knife around edge to release cornbread.

STEWED FRIJOLES

SERVES 8

This recipe can easily be doubled.

- 1 pound dried pinto beans, picked over
- 2 onions, 1 cut into 1/2-inch dice, 1 finely chopped
- 2 garlic cloves, minced
- 1 ham hock (12 ounces)
- 1 can diced tomatoes (28 ounces), with juice
- 3 tablespoons extra-virgin olive oil
- 1/4 cup finely chopped fresh cilantro
- 2 teaspoons coarse salt
- 1/2 teaspoon freshly ground pepper

1. Place beans in a large pot, and add enough cold water to cover by 2 inches. Cover pot; let soak overnight at room temperature.

2. Drain and rinse beans; return to pot, and add diced onion, garlic, ham hock, and tomatoes. Add water to cover by 1 inch. Bring mixture to a boil; reduce heat, and simmer until beans are very tender and most of the liquid has evaporated, 2 1/2 to 3 hours. Remove ham hock; shred meat, and return to pot. Keep warm.

3. Heat oil in a medium skillet over medium heat. Sauté remaining chopped onion, stirring occasionally, until just starting to brown, about 5 minutes. Stir in cilantro, salt, and pepper; cook, stirring, 1 minute. Stir into bean mixture, and serve immediately.

GREEN BEANS AND CHAYOTE WITH TOASTED PINE NUTS

SERVES 8

This recipe can easily be doubled.

- 3 tablespoons extra-virgin olive oil
- 2 chayote squash (about 12 ounces each), peeled and cut into 1/4-inch matchsticks
- 1 1/2 pounds mixed green and yellow string beans, trimmed
- 2 poblano chiles, roasted, ribs and seeds discarded, cut into 1/4-inch-wide strips
- Coarse salt and freshly ground pepper
- Pine nuts, lightly toasted, for garnish

1. Heat 2 tablespoons oil in a sauté pan over medium heat. Add squash; cook, tossing occasionally, until just tender, about 10 minutes. Transfer to a bowl; keep warm.

2. Add remaining tablespoon oil to pan; add string beans, and toss to coat. Add 3 tablespoons water; cover, and cook, stirring occasionally, until bright and crisp-tender, about 10 minutes. Add squash and chiles; stir until heated through. Season with salt and pepper. Serve warm or at room temperature, garnished with pine nuts.

BISCOCHITOS

MAKES 4 DOZEN

- 1 3/4 cups sugar
- 1 1/4 cups lard or solid vegetable shortening
- 1 large egg
- 1 teaspoon pure vanilla extract
- 2 tablespoons Grand Marnier or Triple Sec
- Finely grated zest of 1 orange
- 3 cups all-purpose flour, plus more for work surface
- 1/2 teaspoon baking powder
- 1/4 teaspoon salt
- 2 teaspoons anise seeds
- 1/2 teaspoon ground cinnamon

1. In the bowl of an electric mixer fitted with the paddle attachment, mix 1 cup sugar and the lard on medium-high speed until light and fluffy, about 3 minutes. Add egg; beat to combine. Beat in vanilla, Grand Marnier, and zest.

2. Into a medium bowl, sift together flour, baking powder, and salt. Gradually beat flour mixture into sugar mixture on low speed. Beat in anise seeds. On medium speed, gradually add 2 tablespoons water (or more if needed) to form a ball. Wrap dough in plastic; chill 30 minutes.

3. Preheat oven to 350°F, with rack in center. Line baking sheets with parchment paper. Combine cinnamon and remaining 3/4 cup sugar in a small bowl; set aside. On a floured work surface, roll out dough 1/4 inch thick. Cut dough into crescent moons, stars, or other shapes with a 2-inch cutter; lightly sift cinnamon-sugar over each shape. Place on prepared baking sheets.

4. Bake cookies, one sheet at a time, until firm but not brown, 12 to 14 minutes. Transfer cookies on parchment to a wire rack to cool.

PASTEL DE TRES LECHES

SERVES 12

*This dessert gets its name from the three milks (*tres leches*) that are used to soak the cake. The most time-consuming step is making the coconut curls; you can do this ahead and store them in an airtight container for up to five days at room temperature. In a pinch, toast store-bought shredded coconut.*

- ½ cup (1 stick) unsalted butter, melted and cooled, plus more for pan
- 6 large eggs, separated
- ¼ teaspoon baking soda
- ¼ teaspoon coarse salt
- 1 cup sugar
- 1 cup all-purpose flour
- 2½ cups milk, room temperature
- 1 can evaporated milk (12 ounces)
- 1 can sweetened condensed milk (14 ounces)
- 1 fresh coconut
- 2 cups heavy cream
- Assorted tropical fruits, such as pineapple, star fruit, mango, and papaya, for garnish (optional)

1. Preheat oven to 350°F. Generously butter a 9-by-13-inch metal baking pan. In the bowl of an electric mixer fitted with the whisk attachment, combine egg whites, baking soda, and salt; beat on medium speed until soft peaks form, 2 to 3 minutes. Add yolks; beat until combined. With mixer running, slowly add sugar, beating until combined. Using a rubber spatula, fold in butter.

2. Sift ¼ cup flour on top of egg mixture, and fold in to combine. Repeat with remaining flour, folding in ¼ cup at a time. Pour batter into prepared pan; bake until golden and a cake tester inserted in center comes out clean, 20 to 25 minutes. Transfer pan to a wire rack.

3. Meanwhile, about 5 minutes before cake is finished baking, whisk together the three milks. As soon as the cake is removed from the oven, slowly pour milk mixture over entire cake. (The cake should absorb all the liquid within 3 to 5 minutes.) Let stand until cool. Cover cake with plastic wrap; refrigerate at least 5 hours or overnight.

4. Meanwhile, make coconut curls: Preheat oven to 450°F. Place whole coconut in oven, and bake 20 minutes. Remove from oven. Reduce oven temperature to 375°F. Using a screwdriver, pierce the three eyes of the coconut. Turn over, and drain liquid. Use a hammer to break open coconut. Insert a small spatula or a grapefruit knife between the flesh and the shell to pry the meat out in large pieces. Shave off thin curls of coconut meat with a vegetable peeler. Alternatively, leave shell on and shave off thin curls of meat and shell. Transfer curls to a rimmed baking sheet, and let stand, uncovered, 30 minutes. Bake curls until golden around the edges, about 10 minutes. Set aside to cool.

5. When ready to serve, whip cream to soft peaks. Top slices of cake with whipped cream, and garnish with toasted coconut curls and fruits, as desired.

MAKING AND GARNISHING PASTEL DE TRES LECHES

1. As soon as the sponge cake is removed from the oven, pour the milk mixture over the entire surface. The cake should absorb all the liquid within 3 to 5 minutes. Once cool, refrigerate cake at least 5 hours or overnight.
2. To remove coconut meat from the shell before making curls, insert a small spatula or grapefruit knife between the flesh and the shell of a baked coconut to pry the meat out in large pieces.
3. If you prefer to leave the shell on, you can shave off thin curls of coconut meat and shell using a vegetable peeler (curls will have a brown edge).

RICH CHOCOLATE TART

MAKES ONE 4-BY-14-INCH TART

All-purpose flour, for plastic wrap
Chocolate Dough (recipe follows)
3/4 cup heavy cream
1/4 cup milk
2 tablespoons granulated sugar
7 ounces semisweet chocolate, coarsely chopped
2 large eggs, lightly beaten
1 teaspoon pure hazelnut extract
1 teaspoon pure vanilla extract
4 tablespoons unsweetened cocoa powder

1. Preheat oven to 375°F. On lightly floured plastic wrap or parchment paper, roll out chocolate dough into a 6-by-16-inch rectangle, about 1/8 inch thick. Lifting dough on plastic wrap, flip it over a 4-by-14-inch tart tin, and discard plastic. Fit dough in pan, gently pressing into corners and up sides; trim dough flush with edge. Refrigerate at least 30 minutes.

2. Prick bottom of dough in several places with a fork. Line tin with foil extending about 2 inches over edge; fill with pie weights or dried beans. Bake 20 minutes; remove from oven, and let stand 5 minutes. Remove foil and weights.

3. In a medium saucepan over medium-high heat, cook cream and milk with granulated sugar until just steaming, stirring to dissolve sugar. Place chocolate in a medium heatproof bowl. Pour hot milk mixture over top; whisk gently until chocolate has melted. Gently whisk in eggs and then extracts.

4. Pour chocolate filling into crust; bake until set, 30 to 35 minutes. Let cool in pan on a wire rack.

5. Using a small fine sieve, sift cocoa powder over tart.

CHOCOLATE DOUGH

MAKES ENOUGH FOR ONE 4-BY-14-INCH TART

This dough is very soft; it is best rolled directly on plastic wrap or parchment paper.

1 cup all-purpose flour
2 tablespoons unsweetened cocoa powder
1/4 cup plus 3 tablespoons confectioners' sugar
1/2 cup (1 stick) chilled unsalted butter, cut into small pieces
1 large egg yolk, lightly beaten
1 to 2 tablespoons ice water

In a food processor, pulse flour, cocoa powder, and confectioners' sugar to combine. Add butter, and pulse until mixture resembles coarse meal, about 10 seconds. With machine running, add egg yolk, then 1 to 2 tablespoons ice water; process until dough just begins to come together. Turn out dough onto plastic wrap, and flatten to form a disk; wrap in plastic, and chill at least 1 hour.

MEXICAN HOT CHOCOLATE

SERVES 6 TO 8

1 quart milk
2 whole cinnamon sticks
10 ounces Mexican chocolate, such as Ibarra, finely chopped
Whipped cream, for serving
Ground cinnamon, for serving

Place milk and cinnamon sticks in a large, heavy saucepan. Bring just to a boil; remove from heat. Add chocolate; let stand until chocolate melts, about 3 minutes. Whisk until combined. Remove cinnamon sticks. Serve immediately, topped with whipped cream and a pinch of ground cinnamon.

LATE-AFTERNOON LUNCH *with* FRIENDS

SHRIMP COCKTAIL

SERVES 6

1 lemon, halved
1 fresh or dried bay leaf
2 teaspoons coarse salt
1 1/4 pounds large shrimp (about 3 dozen), peeled and deveined
1 large ripe avocado, pitted, peeled, and sliced into 12 wedges
6 small sprigs basil
Lemon Aïoli, for serving (recipe follows)
Cocktail Sauce, for serving (recipe follows)

1. In a medium saucepan, bring 2 quarts water, lemon, and bay leaf to a boil. Add salt; reduce heat, and simmer 10 minutes. Return to a boil, and stir in shrimp. Cook until bright pink and opaque throughout, 1 1/2 to 2 minutes. Drain; let cool, then refrigerate, covered, until ready to serve, up to 1 day.

2. Divide shrimp and avocado among six dishes; tuck a basil sprig into each. Serve with sauces for dipping.

LEMON AIOLI

MAKES 3/4 CUP

1 small garlic clove
1 large egg
1/2 teaspoon coarse salt, plus more for seasoning
1/2 cup canola oil
1/4 cup extra-virgin olive oil
2 tablespoons freshly squeezed lemon juice
Grated zest of 1 lemon

Pulse garlic in a food processor until finely chopped. Add egg and salt; process until foamy. With machine running, add canola oil and then olive oil in a slow, steady stream through the feed tube. Add lemon juice and zest; pulse to combine. Season with more salt, if desired. Cover with plastic wrap; refrigerate until ready to serve, up to 2 days.

Note: Raw eggs should not be used in food prepared for pregnant women, babies, young children, the elderly, or anyone whose health is compromised.

COCKTAIL SAUCE

MAKES ABOUT 1 CUP

1 cup ketchup
3½ tablespoons prepared horseradish
2 tablespoons freshly squeezed lemon juice
½ teaspoon coarse salt
¼ teaspoon hot-pepper sauce, such as Tabasco

Mix all ingredients in a small bowl. Refrigerate sauce, covered, until ready to serve, up to 3 days.

FRISEE AND BIBB SALAD WITH GARLIC CROUTONS

SERVES 6

1 large garlic clove, minced
1½ large bunches fresh flat-leaf parsley, leaves pulled off and finely chopped
1 loaf Italian bread (about 8 ounces), cut into twelve ½-inch-thick slices
¼ cup plus 6 tablespoons extra-virgin olive oil
Coarse salt
1 head frisée
1 head Bibb lettuce
1 bunch arugula, trimmed
2 tablespoons freshly squeezed lemon juice
Freshly ground pepper

1. Preheat oven to 350°F. Make croutons: Combine garlic and parsley in a small bowl. Brush both sides of bread slices with 6 tablespoons oil. Arrange slices on a baking sheet; sprinkle tops liberally with garlic mixture, and season with salt. Toast, rotating sheet halfway through, until golden and crisp, 18 to 20 minutes. Set aside.

2. Tear frisée and Bibb lettuce into bite-size pieces, and place in a serving bowl along with arugula. In a small bowl, whisk together lemon juice and remaining ¼ cup oil. Drizzle over greens, and season with salt and pepper; toss to combine. Divide salad among six plates; place two croutons on each. Serve immediately.

ROASTED TENDERLOIN AU POIVRE

SERVES 8 TO 10

Ask the butcher to trim off the side piece, silver skin, and all the fat from the filet, reserving one pound of the side piece for the sauce and leaving the filet untied. If you're using beef stock instead of demi-glace, add it to the shallot mixture, and cook until slightly reduced before adding the cream; then proceed with the recipe.

6 pounds beef tenderloin, fully trimmed, 1 pound side piece reserved
¼ cup whole black peppercorns
4 tablespoons olive oil
Coarse salt
⅓ cup finely chopped shallots (about 2 small)
1 teaspoon finely chopped garlic (1 large clove)
1 cup dry red wine
⅓ cup brandy
6 tablespoons demi-glace or unsalted beef stock
¼ cup heavy cream
1 tablespoon finely chopped fresh flat-leaf parsley
½ tablespoon finely chopped fresh rosemary, plus sprigs for garnish
½ tablespoon finely chopped fresh thyme, plus sprigs for garnish

1. Preheat oven to 400°F, with rack in center. Let tenderloin stand at room temperature for 30 minutes. Place peppercorns in a resealable plastic bag; using a meat pounder or mallet, crush peppercorns until coarsely cracked.

2. Rub tenderloin with 2 tablespoons oil; generously season with salt. Firmly press cracked peppercorns into meat with your hands. Transfer to a 12-by-18-inch roasting pan. Set pan over two burners. Sear meat over high heat, turning with tongs as needed, just until each side is brown, about 5 minutes total.

3. Transfer pan to the oven; roast until an instant-read thermometer inserted into thickest part of meat registers 130°F to 140°F (for medium-rare), about 30 minutes. Transfer meat to a cutting board with a well. Tent with foil, and let rest about 20 minutes before slicing.

4. Meanwhile, cut reserved side piece into 1-inch pieces. In a large skillet, heat remaining 2 tablespoons oil over high heat. Add beef; cook, turning often, until browned and cooked through, about 6 minutes. Remove and discard beef. Pour off all but 1 tablespoon oil; reduce heat to low.

5. Add shallots and garlic, and cook until soft and translucent, about 6 minutes. Add wine and brandy; raise heat to high, and cook, stirring up any browned bits with a wooden spoon, until liquid is reduced by two-thirds. Add demi-glace and cream; cook until slightly thickened, about 5 minutes. Season with salt and pepper. Reduce heat to medium; stir in parsley, rosemary, and thyme, and cook 1 minute. Remove from heat; cover, and keep warm.

6. To serve, slice the meat, and transfer to a platter. Garnish with rosemary and thyme, and serve with the sauce.

HARICOTS VERTS WITH HAZELNUTS

SERVES 6

Coarse salt
1 1/4 pounds haricots verts or green beans, stem ends trimmed
1/2 cup hazelnuts (about 2 ounces)
2 tablespoons unsalted butter
Freshly ground pepper

1. Preheat oven to 375°F. Prepare an ice bath; set aside. Bring a large pot of water to a boil; add salt and haricots verts. Cook until beans are bright green and crisp-tender, 3 to 4 minutes. Drain; plunge beans into ice bath to stop the cooking. When completely cool, drain; set aside.

2. Meanwhile, spread hazelnuts in a single layer on a rimmed baking sheet; toast in oven until golden and fragrant, tossing occasionally, about 7 minutes. Remove from oven. Immediately wrap nuts in a clean kitchen towel, and rub them quickly and vigorously to remove as much of the dark, papery skins as possible.

3. In a large skillet, melt butter over medium-high heat. Add beans, and season with salt and pepper. Cook, stirring frequently, until beans are heated through, about 3 minutes. Add hazelnuts; cook, stirring, 1 minute more. Serve warm.

SMASHED RED POTATOES

SERVES 6

You can make the potatoes up to two hours ahead of time; keep them warm by setting the saucepan over a pot of simmering water, keeping pan covered. Mix in the parsley just before serving.

1 1/2 pounds small red new potatoes
Coarse salt
4 tablespoons unsalted butter
1/2 cup half-and-half
Freshly ground pepper
3 tablespoons fresh flat-leaf parsley, coarsely chopped

1. Place potatoes in a 3-quart saucepan. Add enough cold water to cover by about 1 inch. Bring to a boil; add salt. Reduce heat to a simmer; cook until potatoes are tender when pierced with a fork, 20 to 25 minutes. Drain potatoes, and return to pan.

2. Add butter and half-and-half to potatoes; season with salt and pepper. Using a whisk or large fork, lightly smash potatoes, leaving some chunks. Mix in parsley, and season with more salt and pepper, if desired. Serve.

PISTACHIO-CHOCOLATE BUCHE DE NOEL

MAKES ONE 12-INCH LOG

Begin preparing the Chocolate Wood-Grain at the end of step four.

Vegetable-oil cooking spray
5 tablespoons all-purpose flour
5 tablespoons unsweetened cocoa powder, plus more for dusting
1 teaspoon baking powder
1/4 teaspoon salt
5 large eggs, separated, room temperature
3/4 cup sugar
1 teaspoon pure vanilla extract
3 pints pistachio ice cream, beaten until spreadable
Chocolate Wood-Grain (recipe follows)
Chocolate leaves, for garnish (optional)

1. Preheat oven to 350°F. Coat a 12-by-17-inch rimmed baking sheet with cooking spray. Line with parchment paper; spray paper, and set aside. Into a small bowl, sift flour, cocoa, baking powder, and salt.

2. In the bowl of an electric mixer fitted with the whisk attachment, beat yolks and half the sugar until thick and pale. Beat in vanilla. In a clean mixing bowl, beat whites with a clean whisk until soft peaks form. Slowly add remaining sugar; beat until stiff but not dry peaks form. Fold whites into yolk mixture in 3 batches, adding flour mixture with the last batch.

3. Spread batter evenly on prepared baking sheet. Bake until a cake tester inserted in center comes out clean, about 30 minutes. Run a small sharp knife around edges of cake to loosen, and invert onto a clean kitchen towel dusted with cocoa powder. Peel off parchment paper. Starting at a short side, gently roll cake into a log, incorporating towel. Transfer cake to a wire rack to cool completely, about 1 hour.

4. Unroll cake, and spread ice cream evenly over top. Carefully reroll cake (do not incorporate towel). Arrange seam side down on a parchment-lined baking sheet; freeze, covered with plastic, until ice cream is firm, at least 1 hour. Using a hot serrated knife, trim ends of log diagonally.

5. Wrap log in wood-grain: Tuck one end of chocolate-coated acetate under cake while lifting other end up and over cake, being careful not to let chocolate touch cake until sheet is completely surrounding cake and ready to be tucked under at other end. Place cake, seam side down, on inverted baking sheet; return to freezer until chocolate has hardened, about 10 minutes.

6. When ready to serve, remove cake from freezer. Carefully peel acetate from cake, and gently break off ends of chocolate wood-grain to line up with ends of cake.

CHOCOLATE WOOD-GRAIN

MAKES ENOUGH TO COVER ONE 12-INCH LOG

You will need a tool called a graining rocker, used for faux bois, to give the chocolate the appearance of grained wood. You will also need a thin sheet of acetate. Both items are available at hardware and paint-supply stores.

3 ounces white chocolate, melted
6 ounces bittersweet chocolate, finely chopped

1. Cut a thin piece of acetate into a 13½-by-16-inch rectangle. Place on a clean work surface, with a long side facing you. Coat surface of faux-bois tool well with a thick layer of white chocolate. Starting at the right side and working from top to bottom of acetate sheet, rock coated tool back and forth while dragging it in one swift motion to make a vertical striation. Continue until entire sheet is covered in vertical striations. Transfer acetate, chocolate side up, to an inverted rimmed baking sheet; refrigerate until set, about 6 minutes.

2. Meanwhile, temper bittersweet chocolate: Melt two-thirds of chocolate in a heatproof bowl set over a pan of barely simmering water until it registers 118°F on a candy thermometer. Remove pan from heat; add remaining chocolate. Stir with a rubber spatula (avoid using a wooden spoon, which can impart other flavors) until chocolate cools to 84°F. Remove any unmelted pieces, and return bowl to pan; stir until chocolate reaches 88°F to 90°F.

3. Immediately transfer coated acetate to work surface; pour bittersweet chocolate over top. Working quickly, spread chocolate evenly over entire surface with an offset spatula. Try not to spread too much or the white chocolate will smear. Use immediately.

CHOCOLATE LEAVES

MAKES ABOUT 30

Lemon leaves are available at most florists. These chocolate leaves can be refrigerated up to one day.

Pesticide-free lemon leaves
6 ounces bittersweet chocolate, finely chopped

1. Gently clean the leaves with a damp paper towel. Let dry on a baking sheet.

2. Line a baking sheet with parchment paper, and set aside. Heat two-thirds of chocolate in a heatproof bowl set over a pan of barely simmering water until chocolate registers 118°F on a candy thermometer. Remove bowl from heat; add remaining chocolate, and stir with a rubber spatula (avoid using a wooden spoon, which can impart other flavors) until chocolate cools to 84°F. Remove any unmelted pieces; discard, and return bowl to pan. Stir until chocolate reaches 88°F to 90°F.

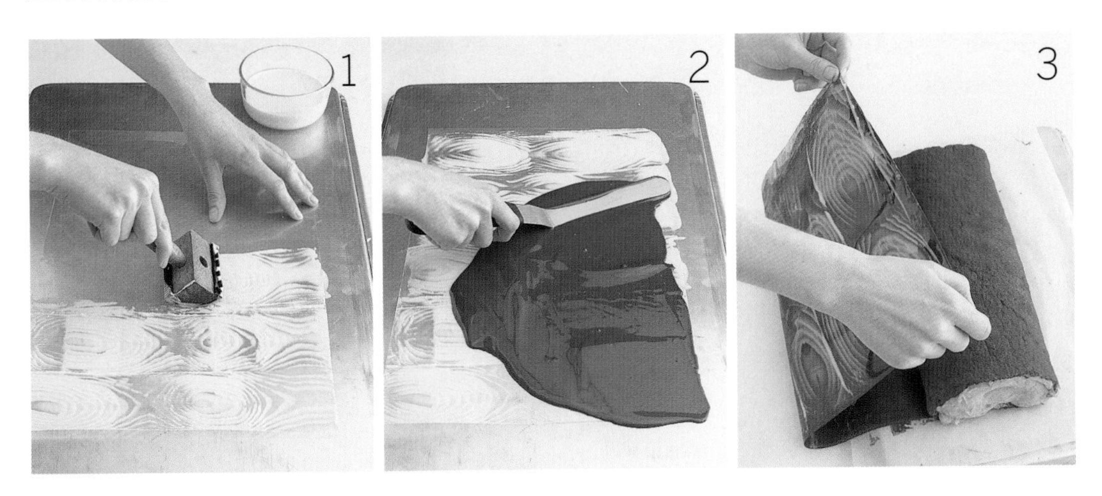

MAKING CHOCOLATE WOOD-GRAIN

1. Coat a wood-graining rocker with a thick layer of melted white chocolate. Paint stripes on a 13½-by-16-inch piece of acetate (plastic wrap is not stiff enough to use), rocking the tool back and forth while dragging it in one swift motion. Refrigerate until set, about 6 minutes.

2. Pour bittersweet chocolate over white-chocolate wood-grain. Using an offset spatula, quickly but gently spread the dark chocolate over the entire surface, keeping the white chocolate intact.

3. Drape the acetate, chocolate side down, over the frozen bûche de Noël. Have someone help you keep the chocolate from touching the log until it is draped smoothly around the whole log. Place cake, seam side down, on a baking sheet, and freeze until chocolate is hardened, at least 10 minutes. When ready to serve, carefully peel off acetate, and gently break off excess chocolate shell so it lines up with edges of log.

3. Using a pastry brush, paint veiny underside of leaves generously with chocolate, covering entire surface. Place painted leaves, chocolate side up, on prepared baking sheet. Refrigerate the leaves until chocolate is firm, about 10 minutes.

4. Starting from stem ends, carefully peel leaves from chocolate, and discard leaves. Transfer chocolate leaves to a clean parchment-lined baking sheet, and refrigerate until ready to use.

VANILLA-BEAN BUTTER COOKIES

MAKES ABOUT 5 DOZEN

- 1 cup (2 sticks) unsalted butter, room temperature
- 1⅓ cups confectioners' sugar
- 3 vanilla beans, split lengthwise
- 1 large egg
- ½ teaspoon pure vanilla extract
- 2½ cups sifted all-purpose flour, plus more for work surface
- ¼ teaspoon salt
- Colored small round dragées (optional)
- Sanding sugar, for sprinkling

1. Combine butter and confectioners' sugar in the bowl of an electric mixer fitted with the paddle attachment. Scrape in vanilla seeds. Beat on high speed until fluffy, 2 to 3 minutes. Add egg and vanilla extract; beat to combine. Add flour and salt; beat on low speed until incorporated. Divide dough in half; flatten into disks. Wrap in plastic, and refrigerate at least 1 hour or overnight.

2. Preheat oven to 350°F. On a lightly floured work surface, roll out both dough disks to ¼ inch thick. Place dough on separate baking sheets, and transfer to freezer or refrigerator until chilled, about 20 minutes.

3. Line several baking sheets with parchment paper. Remove dough from freezer. Using a 2-inch star-shaped cookie cutter, cut out stars; place them 1 inch apart on prepared sheets. Place a dragée in center of each star, if desired; sprinkle generously with sanding sugar. Freeze or refrigerate until firm, 10 to 20 minutes.

4. Bake until golden, rotating baking sheets halfway through, 18 to 22 minutes. Transfer to wire racks to cool completely.

CRANBERRY-CITRUS PUNCH

SERVES ABOUT 20

You will need twenty wooden skewers to make the cranberry-mint swizzle sticks.

- 1 bag fresh whole cranberries (12 ounces), for swizzle sticks (optional)
- 1 bunch mint leaves, for swizzle sticks (optional)
- 5 cups cranberry-juice cocktail
- 3 cups freshly squeezed tangerine juice (about 7 tangerines)
- 2 cups freshly squeezed pomegranate juice (about 5 pomegranates)
- 2 bottles (750 ml each) sparkling wine

1. Make swizzle sticks, if desired: Spear 3 cranberries alternately with 2 mint leaves on each of 20 wooden skewers. Place on a baking sheet; cover with damp paper towels. Refrigerate up to 1 hour.

2. In a large punch bowl, stir together fruit juices. Fill glasses with ice. Ladle about ½ cup punch into each glass, then top with sparkling wine. Garnish with swizzle sticks.

ROASTED ALMONDS WITH OLIVE OIL

MAKES ABOUT 2 CUPS

- 2 cups whole blanched almonds (about 8 ounces)
- 1½ tablespoons extra-virgin olive oil
- 1 teaspoon coarse sea salt

Preheat oven to 350°F. Spread almonds in a single layer on a rimmed baking sheet; toast in oven until golden, tossing occasionally, about 15 minutes. Let cool completely. Transfer to a bowl. Add oil and salt, and toss to combine. Store in an airtight container at room temperature up to 2 days.

CROSTINI WITH SMOKED TROUT

SERVES 20

These crostini are made with a wreath-shaped loaf of peasant bread, found in artisanal bakeries and gourmet food shops. You can also use a round loaf with the center cut out.

- 1 pound boneless smoked trout fillets, skins removed
- 4 ounces cream cheese, room temperature
- 4 ounces crème fraîche
- ¼ cup prepared horseradish
- ¼ cup freshly squeezed lemon juice (about 2 lemons)
- Freshly ground pepper
- 1 loaf peasant bread (1 to 1½ pounds)
- Extra-virgin olive oil, for brushing
- 1 bunch watercress, tough stems removed
- 6 ounces cherry tomatoes, halved
- 1 kirby cucumber, halved lengthwise and thinly sliced crosswise into half-moons

1. Preheat oven to 375°F. In a food processor, pulse trout fillets several times until broken up into small pieces. In a medium bowl, whisk together cream cheese, crème fraîche, horseradish, and lemon juice. Fold in trout, and season with pepper. Cover with plastic; refrigerate until ready to use, up to 2 days.

2. Using a long serrated knife, trim off top of loaf to make level. Cut bread into ¾-inch-thick slices, keeping shape of loaf intact. Brush top with oil. Arrange loaf, oiled side up, on a baking sheet; toast until golden brown, about 12 minutes. Let cool.

3. Transfer toasted bread loaf to a serving platter. Spread trout mixture on bread. Arrange watercress, tomatoes, and cucumber on top. Serve immediately.

ROASTED TURKEY BREAST WITH FENNEL-HERB STUFFING

SERVES 6 TO 8

This recipe can be doubled or tripled to serve larger groups.

- 4 tablespoons unsalted butter
- 1 yellow onion, finely chopped
- 2 garlic cloves, minced
- 1 small fennel bulb, trimmed and finely chopped
- 11 slices (1/2 inch thick) country bread, trimmed of crusts and cut into 1/2-inch cubes (about 5 cups)
- 1 tablespoon fresh thyme leaves
- 2 tablespoons coarsely chopped fresh rosemary, plus sprigs for garnish
- 1/2 cup coarsely chopped fresh flat-leaf parsley
- 2 1/4 to 3 1/4 cups homemade or low-sodium store-bought chicken broth
- Coarse salt and freshly ground pepper
- 1 whole boneless turkey breast (6 pounds)
- 2 tablespoons extra-virgin olive oil
- 1 blood orange, thinly sliced, for garnish (optional)

1. Melt butter in a large skillet over medium heat. Add onion and garlic; cook, stirring occasionally, until onion is soft and translucent, about 4 minutes. Add fennel, and cook, stirring, until tender, about 4 minutes. Transfer mixture to a large bowl. Stir in bread, thyme, rosemary, parsley, and 1 1/4 cups stock. Season with salt and pepper. Set stuffing aside.

2. Preheat oven to 375°F. Place turkey, skin side down, on a clean work surface. Using a sharp knife, remove tenderloins. To butterfly turkey, slice vertically through right side of breast, starting at thickest part and slicing almost to edge without cutting through (it should resemble a book, with a flap in the center). Spread open; gently press down to flatten. Repeat on left side. Cover with plastic wrap. Using a meat mallet or heavy skillet, pound meat until uniform in thickness.

3. Season turkey with salt and pepper, then spread stuffing down center lengthwise. Fold both sides of turkey over stuffing. Using kitchen twine, tie turkey at 1-inch intervals to completely encase stuffing and form a long cylinder.

4. Transfer turkey to a roasting rack in a roasting pan. Pour 1 cup stock into bottom of pan. Brush turkey with oil, and season with salt and pepper. Roast, basting with pan juices every 30 minutes (add remaining cup stock if pan gets too dry), until well browned and an instant-read thermometer inserted into thickest part of turkey registers 165°F, about 1 3/4 hours. If skin begins to get too dark, tent pan with foil. Transfer turkey to a carving board, and let rest 20 minutes before slicing. Garnish with orange slices, if desired, and rosemary sprigs.

SMOKED HAM WITH MAPLE GLAZE

SERVES 15 TO 20

Remove the ham from the refrigerator one to two hours before baking so it will come to room temperature.

- 1 smoked bone-in ham (10 to 12 pounds), room temperature
- 1/2 cup apricot jam
- 2 tablespoons Dijon mustard
- 3/4 cup pure maple syrup
- 2 tablespoons dark rum
- 1 garlic clove, minced
- Fresh bay leaves, for garnish (optional)
- Kumquats, for garnish (optional)

1. Preheat oven to 350°F. Place ham on a roasting rack in a large roasting pan; cover tightly with foil. Bake 4 hours, rotating pan halfway through.

2. Meanwhile, make glaze: In a small saucepan, heat jam until liquefied. Strain through a fine sieve into a small bowl; discard solids. Stir in mustard, maple syrup, rum, and garlic.

3. After 4 hours, remove ham from oven, and brush with glaze. Continue baking, glazing every 15 minutes, until an instant-read thermometer inserted into thickest part of ham (avoiding bone) registers 140°F, about 1 hour more. Remove ham from oven; transfer to a carving board or platter. Garnish with bay leaves and kumquats, if desired. Slice thinly around bone, and serve hot or at room temperature.

GRAPEFRUIT AND CRANBERRY CHUTNEY

MAKES ABOUT 3 CUPS

- 12 ounces fresh or frozen (thawed) cranberries
- 3/4 cup sugar
- 2 tablespoons cider vinegar
- 1/4 teaspoon ground cardamom
- Pinch of ground cloves
- Pinch of salt
- 1/2 cup dried sour cherries
- 2 ruby-red grapefruits, pith and peel removed, separated into sections

In a small saucepan, combine cranberries, sugar, vinegar, cardamom, cloves, and salt. Stir to combine. Place over medium heat; cook, stirring constantly, until cranberries just begin to burst and soften, about 5 minutes. Turn off heat; stir in cherries, and transfer to a medium bowl. Let cool completely, then gently mix in grapefruit. Cover with plastic wrap; refrigerate chutney until ready to serve, up to 5 days.

BUTTERNUT SQUASH CRUMBLE

SERVES 8

You can make this recipe through step two up to one day in advance; refrigerate, covered with plastic wrap. The crumb topping can also be made one day in advance; store separately in an airtight container in the refrigerator.

- 3/4 cup (1 1/2 sticks) chilled unsalted butter, cut into 1/2-inch pieces, plus more for dish
- 3 tablespoons extra-virgin olive oil
- 3 small butternut squash (about 4 pounds), peeled, seeded, and cut into 3/4-inch chunks
- Coarse salt and freshly ground pepper
- 2 large shallots, thinly sliced
- 1/4 cup coarsely chopped fresh flat-leaf parsley
- 1/2 cup homemade or low-sodium store-bought chicken broth
- 1 1/2 cups all-purpose flour
- 3/4 teaspoon sugar
- 2 tablespoons fresh thyme leaves
- 1 teaspoon table salt
- 2 large egg yolks
- 3 or 4 tablespoons ice water

1. Preheat oven to 375°F. Generously butter a 9-by-2-inch square baking dish; set aside. Heat 1 tablespoon oil in a large skillet over medium-high heat. Add half the squash, and season with coarse salt and pepper. Cook, stirring occasionally, until well browned, 8 to 10 minutes. Transfer to prepared dish. Repeat with another tablespoon oil and the remaining squash.

2. Reduce heat to medium; add remaining tablespoon oil and the shallots to skillet. Cook, stirring frequently, until shallots are lightly browned, 3 to 5 minutes. Transfer to baking dish along with parsley and stock; stir to combine. Cover dish tightly with foil; bake, stirring occasionally, until squash is just tender, about 30 minutes.

3. Meanwhile, place flour, sugar, thyme, and table salt in a food processor; pulse to combine. Add butter, and process until mixture resembles coarse meal. Whisk together yolks and 3 tablespoons ice water in a small bowl; add to flour mixture. Pulse until mixture forms pea-size crumbs. If dough is too dry, add remaining tablespoon ice water.

4. Remove squash from oven. Arrange crumb mixture on top. Return to oven, and bake until topping is golden brown and squash is very tender, about 30 minutes. Transfer to a wire rack to cool. Serve warm or at room temperature.

GREEN BEANS WITH SHIITAKE MUSHROOMS

SERVES 6 TO 8

- Coarse salt
- 1½ pounds green beans, stem ends trimmed
- ½ cup extra-virgin olive oil, plus more as needed
- ¾ pound fresh shiitake mushrooms, stemmed, wiped clean, and thinly sliced
- Freshly ground pepper

1. Bring a large saucepan of water to a boil; add salt. Prepare an ice bath; set aside. Working in two batches, cook green beans in boiling water until crisp-tender, 3 to 5 minutes. Using a slotted spoon, plunge beans into ice bath to stop the cooking. Drain, and pat dry; set aside.

2. Heat oil in a large skillet over high heat until hot but not smoking. Working in batches so as not to crowd skillet, add mushrooms; season with salt and pepper. Cook, stirring frequently, until mushrooms are golden and crisp, 2 to 3 minutes. Using a slotted spoon, transfer mushrooms to paper towels to drain. Add more oil as needed for subsequent batches.

3. Reduce heat to medium. Add beans, and season with salt and pepper. Cook, tossing, until beans are heated through, about 3 minutes. Transfer to a large serving dish. Add mushrooms, and toss to combine. Serve warm or at room temperature.

GREEN SALAD WITH WALNUTS AND DATE VINAIGRETTE

SERVES 6 TO 8

- 1 cup walnut halves (4 ounces)
- 5 ounces dates, pitted
- 1 teaspoon Dijon mustard
- ½ cup cider vinegar
- ½ cup extra-virgin olive oil
- Coarse salt and freshly ground pepper
- 1 head green-leaf lettuce (about 10 ounces), leaves torn
- 3 heads Belgian endive (about 12 ounces), leaves torn
- 1 bunch baby spinach (about 4 ounces)
- 1 head red Bibb lettuce (about 8 ounces)

1. Preheat oven to 350°F. Spread walnuts in a single layer on a rimmed baking sheet; toast in oven until fragrant, tossing occasionally, 10 to 12 minutes. Let cool.

2. In a food processor, pulse 5 of the dates with the mustard and vinegar until puréed. With machine running, slowly pour oil through the feed tube until emulsified. Season with salt and pepper.

3. Quarter remaining dates lengthwise. In a large bowl, combine greens, quartered dates, and walnuts; drizzle with dressing, and toss to combine. Serve.

CHEDDAR CHEESE AND SAGE BISCUITS

MAKES ABOUT 16

- 4 cups all-purpose flour, plus more for work surface
- 4 teaspoons baking powder
- 1 teaspoon baking soda
- 1 teaspoon salt
- 1 teaspoon sugar
- ½ teaspoon paprika
- 1 cup (2 sticks) chilled unsalted butter, cut into small pieces
- 3 cups grated cheddar cheese (9 ounces)
- ⅔ cup thinly sliced fresh sage leaves
- 2 cups buttermilk
- 1 large egg, lightly beaten
- 1 tablespoon heavy cream

1. Preheat oven to 375°F. In a medium bowl, whisk together flour, baking powder, baking soda, salt, sugar, and paprika. Using a pastry blender or two knives, cut in butter until mixture resembles coarse crumbs. Stir in cheese and sage. Add buttermilk; stir with a fork until mixture just comes together to form a sticky dough. On a lightly floured work surface, with floured hands, pat dough into a 1-inch-thick round.

2. Using a 2½-inch biscuit or cookie cutter, cut out biscuits as close together as possible, dipping cutter into flour to prevent sticking. Transfer biscuits to a baking sheet.

3. In a small bowl, stir together egg and cream; lightly brush egg wash over top of each biscuit. Bake until golden brown, rotating baking sheet halfway through, 20 to 30 minutes. Transfer to a wire rack. Serve warm or at room temperature.

RUM BALLS

MAKES ABOUT 4 DOZEN

These chocolate balls are made by baking a brownie and then processing it into crumbs; rum is added to bind the crumbs together. The balls can be refrigerated in an airtight container for up to two days.

Vegetable-oil cooking spray
3/4 cup (1 1/2 sticks) unsalted butter
6 ounces semisweet chocolate, finely chopped
3 large eggs
1/2 cup packed light-brown sugar
1 teaspoon pure vanilla extract
1/2 teaspoon salt
3/4 cup all-purpose flour
1/4 cup plus 2 tablespoons dark rum
Red sanding sugar, for rolling

1. Preheat oven to 350°F. Coat a 12-by-17-inch rimmed baking sheet with cooking spray; set aside. Combine butter and chocolate in a small heatproof bowl set over a pan of simmering water, stirring occasionally, until chocolate is melted and mixture is smooth and combined.

2. In a large bowl, whisk together eggs, brown sugar, vanilla, and salt. Stir in chocolate mixture, then fold in flour. Pour batter onto prepared baking sheet; spread evenly with an offset spatula. Bake until top is shiny, rotating sheet halfway through, about 10 minutes (do not overbake; a cake tester should come out with some crumbs attached). Let cool completely.

3. Break up brownie into small pieces, and place in the bowl of an electric mixer fitted with the paddle attachment. With machine on low, slowly pour rum into bowl; mix until crumbs start to come together to form a ball.

4. Shape mixture into 1-inch balls. Roll in sanding sugar, coating completely. Place on a baking sheet; refrigerate, uncovered, until chilled, about 2 hours.

GINGER CHEESECAKE BARS

MAKES ABOUT 4 DOZEN

Vegetable-oil cooking spray
12 ounces gingersnaps
4 tablespoons unsalted butter, melted
12 ounces cream cheese, room temperature
3/4 cup sugar
1 large whole egg
1 large egg yolk
3 tablespoons sour cream
3/4 teaspoon pure vanilla extract
2 tablespoons finely chopped crystallized ginger

1. Preheat oven to 350°F. Coat a 9-by-13-inch baking pan with cooking spray; set aside. Place gingersnaps in a food processor; pulse to a powder. Transfer to a small bowl, and stir in butter until well combined. Press gingersnap mixture evenly into bottom of prepared baking pan. Bake until firm, about 12 minutes. Let cool completely.

2. Meanwhile, in the bowl of an electric mixer fitted with the paddle attachment, beat cream cheese until smooth and softened. Beat in sugar, egg, egg yolk, sour cream, and vanilla until well combined. Beat in crystallized ginger.

3. Pour cream-cheese mixture onto crust, and spread evenly to edges. Bake, rotating baking pan halfway through, until filling has puffed and feels slightly firm to the touch (don't let it brown), about 25 minutes. Transfer to a wire rack to cool completely. Refrigerate, covered with plastic wrap, until chilled and set, at least 1 hour and up to 2 days. To serve, cut into bars with a serrated knife.

MAPLE SHORTBREAD WITH PECANS

MAKES ABOUT 2 DOZEN

Turbinado sugar, which has a golden color, can be found in many supermarkets; sanding sugar is a fine substitute.

2 1/4 cups all-purpose flour, plus more for work surface
1/2 cup cake flour (not self-rising)
1/2 teaspoon salt
3/4 cup pecan halves, finely chopped (about 3 ounces)
1 cup (2 sticks) unsalted butter, room temperature
3/4 cup granulated sugar
1/4 cup pure maple syrup
1 large egg yolk
1/4 teaspoon pure maple extract
1 large whole egg, lightly beaten
Turbinado sugar, for sprinkling

1. Line a large baking sheet with parchment paper, and set aside. Into a medium bowl, sift together flours and salt. Whisk in 1/2 cup chopped pecans; set aside.

2. In the bowl of an electric mixer fitted with the paddle attachment, cream butter and sugar on medium speed until smooth and light, about 1 minute. Add maple syrup, egg yolk, and extract; beat until well combined. With mixer on low, gradually add flour mixture, beating until just combined. Dough should be smooth and pliable. Flatten dough into a disk. Wrap in plastic; chill until firm, 1 1/2 hours or overnight.

3. Preheat oven to 350°F. On a lightly floured work surface, roll out dough to 1/4 inch thick. Cut out rounds using a 2-inch cookie cutter; place rounds 1 inch apart on prepared baking sheet. Brush tops with beaten egg; sprinkle centers with remaining 1/4 cup pecans, dividing evenly. Sprinkle entire surface with turbinado sugar.

4. Bake cookies until golden around the edges, rotating baking sheet halfway through, 10 to 12 minutes. Transfer cookies to a wire rack to cool completely. Store in an airtight container at room temperature up to 4 days.

COCONUT-CRANBERRY COOKIES

MAKES 3 DOZEN

- 3 cups all-purpose flour
- 1 teaspoon baking powder
- 1/4 teaspoon salt
- 1 1/2 cups (3 sticks) unsalted butter, room temperature
- 1 3/4 cups sugar
- 2 teaspoons pure vanilla extract
- Grated zest of 1 navel orange
- 1 1/2 cups dried cranberries
- 1 1/2 cups sweetened shredded coconut

1. Preheat oven to 350°F. Line two large baking sheets with parchment paper; set aside. In a medium bowl, whisk together flour, baking powder, and salt; set aside.

2. In the bowl of an electric mixer fitted with the paddle attachment, beat butter, sugar, vanilla, and orange zest on medium speed until creamy and light. Add flour mixture, and beat on medium-low speed until mixture comes together to form a dough. Beat in cranberries and coconut.

3. Shape dough into 1 1/4-inch balls, and place them 2 inches apart on prepared baking sheets. Flatten each ball slightly. Bake until edges begin to brown, rotating baking sheets halfway through, 15 to 17 minutes. Let cool on baking sheets 5 minutes, then transfer to wire racks to cool completely.

PEAR TART

MAKES ONE 4-BY-13-INCH TART

- 3/4 cup whole blanched almonds (about 3 ounces)
- 1/2 cup (1 stick) unsalted butter, room temperature
- 1/2 cup sugar, plus more for sprinkling
- 1 large egg
- 2 tablespoons heavy cream
- 1/4 teaspoon pure almond extract
- Almond Tart Shell (recipe follows)
- 1 ripe but firm red Bartlett or Comice pear, cored and cut into 1/4-inch-thick slices
- Vanilla-Bean Crème Anglaise, for serving (recipe follows)

1. Preheat oven to 350°F. Spread almonds in a single layer on a rimmed baking sheet; toast in oven until lightly golden, tossing occasionally, about 10 minutes. Let cool completely, then finely grind in a food processor. Set aside.

2. In the bowl of an electric mixer fitted with the paddle attachment, cream butter and sugar on medium speed until smooth and light, about 1 minute. Add almonds, egg, cream, and extract; beat until well combined, about 2 minutes.

3. Using a small offset spatula, spread filling in cooled tart shell. Arrange pear slices on top of filling down length of tart, slightly overlapping. Generously sprinkle sugar over top, and place tart on a baking sheet. Bake until filling is slightly puffed and golden brown, about 35 minutes. Transfer to a wire rack to cool. Serve warm or at room temperature with crème anglaise on the side.

ALMOND TART SHELL

MAKES ONE 4-BY-13-INCH SHELL

- 1/4 cup whole blanched almonds (about 1 ounce)
- 1 cup plus 2 teaspoons all-purpose flour, plus more for work surface
- 1/4 teaspoon baking soda
- 1/8 teaspoon salt
- 1/2 cup (1 stick) unsalted butter, room temperature
- 1/2 cup sugar
- 1 large egg yolk
- 1/4 teaspoon pure vanilla extract

1. Preheat oven to 350°F. Spread almonds in a single layer on a rimmed baking sheet; toast in oven until lightly golden, tossing occasionally, about 10 minutes. Let cool completely, then finely grind in a food processor. Set aside.

2. In a small bowl, whisk together flour, baking soda, and salt; set aside. In the bowl of an electric mixer fitted with the paddle attachment, cream butter and sugar on medium speed until smooth and light, about 1 minute. Add almonds, egg yolk, and extract; beat until well combined. With mixer on low speed, gradually add flour mixture, beating until just combined. Turn out dough onto a piece of plastic wrap; pat into a flattened rectangle. Wrap in plastic, and refrigerate until firm, at least 1 hour or overnight.

3. Reheat oven to 350°F. On a lightly floured work surface, roll out dough to a 6-by-16-inch rectangle, about 3/8 inch thick. Fit dough into a 4-by-13-inch rectangular tart pan with a removable bottom, pressing dough into bottom and up sides. Trim dough flush with edge of pan. Prick bottom of dough all over with a fork. Freeze or refrigerate until firm, about 15 minutes.

4. Place tart pan on a baking sheet; bake until crust starts to brown around the edges, 13 to 14 minutes (dough will be slightly puffed in spots). Transfer to a wire rack. Using a metal spatula, gently press on dough until it is smooth and flat. Let cool completely.

VANILLA-BEAN CREME ANGLAISE

MAKES ABOUT 2 CUPS

- 4 large egg yolks
- 1/4 cup sugar
- Pinch of salt
- 1 cup milk
- 3/4 cup heavy cream
- 1 vanilla bean, split lengthwise and scraped

1. Prepare an ice bath; set aside. In the bowl of an electric mixer, whisk together egg yolks, sugar, and salt on high speed until pale yellow and very thick.

2. Meanwhile, in a small saucepan, bring milk, cream, and vanilla bean and scrapings just to a boil. Remove from heat.

3. With mixer on low speed, gradually pour half the hot milk mixture into yolk mixture. Return mixture to saucepan. Cook over medium-low heat, stirring constantly with a wooden spoon, until mixture is thick enough to coat back of spoon and hold a line drawn by your finger on the spoon, about 5 minutes. Pass mixture through a fine sieve into a bowl. Place bowl in the ice bath, stirring occasionally, until chilled. Use immediately, or refrigerate, covered, up to 3 days. Whisk gently before using.

NEW YEAR'S EVE DINNER *in* THE CITY

SHRIMP AND GREEN PEA RISOTTO

SERVES 6 TO 8

The risotto will continue to thicken slightly after being removed from the heat, so be careful not to overcook it.

- 3 bottles (8 ounces each) clam juice
- 3 tablespoons olive oil
- 5 garlic cloves, minced
- 3 medium leeks, white and pale-green parts only, finely chopped and washed well (1 1/2 cups)
- 1 1/2 cups Arborio rice
- Coarse salt and freshly ground pepper
- 3/4 cup dry white wine
- Grated zest and juice of 1 lemon
- 1 pound medium shrimp, peeled and deveined
- 1 cup frozen green peas, thawed
- 1/4 cup finely chopped fresh flat-leaf parsley
- 4 tablespoons unsalted butter

1. In a medium saucepan, bring clam juice and 3 cups water to a bare simmer. Heat oil in a large, heavy-bottom saucepan over medium heat. Add garlic; cook, stirring often, until soft, about 3 minutes. Add leeks; cook, stirring often, until soft, about 4 minutes. Add rice; cook, stirring, until grains are coated with oil and translucent around edges, 3 to 4 minutes. Season with salt and pepper.

2. Add wine and lemon zest; cook, stirring constantly, until almost all wine is absorbed, about 1 minute. Ladle 3/4 cup hot clam broth into pan. Using a wooden spoon, stir constantly over medium heat, reducing heat if needed to maintain a gentle simmer, until rice has absorbed most of the liquid and mixture is just thick enough to leave a wake behind the spoon when stirred.

3. Continue adding broth 3/4 cup at a time and stirring constantly, until rice is mostly translucent but still opaque and slightly crunchy in the center, a total of 20 to 25 minutes; add shrimp and peas with the last addition of broth, stirring until they are cooked through (3 to 4 minutes). As the rice nears doneness, watch carefully, and add smaller amounts of the hot broth. The mixture should be thick enough that grains of rice are suspended in liquid that is the consistency of heavy cream.

4. Stir in parsley, lemon juice, and butter. Season risotto again with salt and pepper, and serve immediately.

CHEESE GLOSSARY

On New Year's Eve, Eric Pike serves a selection of sheep's and goat's milk cheeses. Consider any of the following when planning a party:

1. NOORD (HOLLAND)
This dark yellow sheep's milk cheese is particularly strong-tasting, almost earthy.

2. HUMBOLDT FOG (UNITED STATES)
A semi-aged, creamy goat cheese from California, Humboldt Fog is distinguished by a line of vegetable ash that runs through its center.

3. RICOTTA SALATA (ITALY)
A subtle, slightly salty sheep's milk cheese perfect for those who dislike strong tastes. Ricotta salata has no rind and is semi-firm in texture.

4. MANCHEGO (SPAIN)
A popular semi-firm sheep's milk cheese, the variety shown here (sasenado) is spicy—seasoned with red and black pepper and rosemary.

5. JACQUIN BLUTTE (FRANCE)
Triangular in shape, this pungent blue cheese, made from goat's milk, is especially delicious with red wine.

6. LINGOT DU QUERCY (FRANCE)
Similar in taste to Camembert, this full-flavored semi-aged goat's milk cheese is soft and spreadable.

7. LE CHEVROT (FRANCE)
A good goat cheese for beginners, Le Chevrot is smooth, rich, buttery, and tangy all at once.

8. P'TIT BASQUE (FRANCE)
A smooth, semi-firm cheese redolent of the flavor of sheep's milk, it pairs well with Muscat grapes.

CAVIAR GLOSSARY

Possibly the quintessential luxury food, caviar strikes the perfect celebratory note for an occasion such as Christmas or New Year's Eve. Here are the most recognizable varieties.

AMERICAN GOLDEN WHITEFISH
The small, crunchy, slightly bitter roe of the whitefish makes an excellent topping for cooked potatoes, with or without sour cream.

AMERICAN STURGEON
The eggs of the paddlefish, a relative of the sturgeon, are harvested in the Tennessee River basin; quality is at its best, variable, but this caviar can almost pass for beluga, at less than a third the cost.

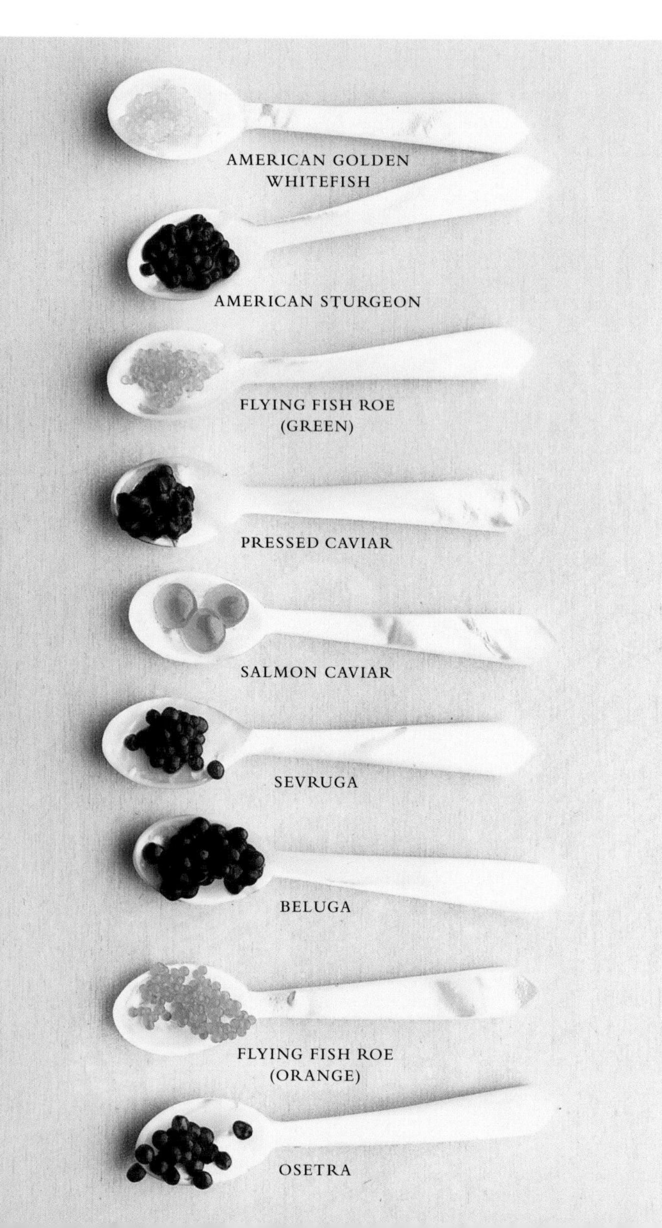

FLYING FISH ROE (GREEN)
This is a variety of the orange flying-fish roe (see below) that is tinted green by wasabi, the pungent Japanese horseradish.

PRESSED CAVIAR
Thick and jamlike, it is made of eggs that were broken in processing. It has a very intense flavor that can be an acquired taste. It is best eaten diluted by something mild like sour cream and spread on something substantial and crunchy, such as a crisp potato pancake.

SALMON CAVIAR
These beautiful, large, reddish orange eggs tend to be saltier than those of the sturgeon, and the flavor is less complex. But at less than $40 a pound, they can be heaped in a bowl for guests to spoon up with abandon, or to spread on a toasted, thinly sliced bagel with cream cheese for a New Year's Day brunch.

SEVRUGA
The smallest (and least expensive) of the Caspian Sea sturgeon caviars, it is the choice of many connoisseurs for its sweet, almost fruity flavor and firm texture.

BELUGA
The queen of caviars, with large, elegant, mild-tasting eggs that burst on the tongue with a taste of the ocean. Serve with tiny spoons, preferably made of mother-of-pearl.

FLYING FISH ROE (ORANGE)
Used in sushi, these small, crunchy eggs have a mild flavor and are good as a garnish or spread in a thin layer on a buttered cracker.

OSETRA
In size and price intermediate between sevruga and beluga, these light- to dark-brown eggs typically have a more assertive flavor than either of the other types. Wonderful with crème fraîche on warm blini.

ROASTED PEAR AND SHALLOT SALAD WITH SHERRY-DIJON VINAIGRETTE

SERVES 6 TO 8

- 2 tablespoons honey
- 5 tablespoons sherry vinegar
- 5 tablespoons olive oil
- Coarse salt and freshly ground pepper
- 3 Bosc pears, cored, each cut into eighths (unpeeled)
- 8 shallots, halved lengthwise if large
- 1 teaspoon Dijon mustard
- 1 large head frisée (about 8 ounces), trimmed and leaves separated
- 2 heads endive, leaves separated and torn in half if large
- ¾ cup walnut halves, toasted

1. Preheat oven to 400°F. In a medium bowl, whisk together honey, 3 tablespoons vinegar, and 2 tablespoons oil; season with salt and pepper. Arrange pears and shallots in a single layer in a roasting pan; pour honey mixture over top, and toss well to coat. Cook 20 minutes; check for browning, turning pears and shallots if needed. Continue cooking until shallots are easily pierced with the tip of a paring knife, about 10 minutes more.

2. Meanwhile, make vinaigrette: In a small bowl, whisk together remaining 2 tablespoons vinegar, 3 tablespoons oil, and mustard; season with salt and pepper. Set aside.

3. Remove roasted pears and shallots. Place roasting pan over high heat; add ⅓ cup water, and scrape up any browned bits from bottom of pan with a wooden spoon. Let liquid reduce by half, then whisk mixture into vinaigrette.

4. Combine frisée and endive in a large bowl; toss with the vinaigrette. Divide among serving plates, and arrange pears, shallots, and walnuts alongside. Serve.

GRASSHOPPER TARTS

MAKES 6 SMALL TARTS

These desserts are named for the classic cocktail, which is made with crème de menthe.

- ¾ cup sugar
- 3½ tablespoons crème de menthe
- ¼ teaspoon pure spearmint extract
- 1 teaspoon unflavored gelatin
- 2½ cups heavy cream
- 2 cups loosely packed fresh mint leaves, plus 6 sprigs for garnish
- 5 large egg yolks
- 1 large whole egg
- 3 ounces semisweet chocolate, finely chopped, plus a few shavings for garnish
- Chocolate-Wafer Crusts (recipe follows)

1. Combine sugar and ½ cup water in a small saucepan over medium-high heat; stir until sugar is dissolved. Remove from heat; let cool slightly. Stir in crème de menthe and spearmint extract. Sprinkle gelatin over top; let soften, about 5 minutes.

2. Heat 1½ cups cream in another small saucepan until it is almost at a boil. Turn off heat, and add mint; cover, and let steep 10 minutes.

3. Prepare an ice bath; set aside. Whisk egg yolks and egg in a heatproof bowl. Strain cream mixture through a fine sieve into egg mixture; place bowl over a pan of simmering water. Add gelatin mixture, and whisk constantly until mixture begins to thicken and registers 160°F on a candy thermometer. Transfer bowl to ice bath; stir occasionally until mixture is cool.

4. In a medium bowl, whisk remaining cup cream to soft peaks. Gently whisk in mint mixture, and fold in chocolate pieces. Fill crusts with mixture, dividing evenly. Transfer rings to refrigerator until filling is set, at least 2 hours. To unmold, warm each ring in your hands, and shake gently until tart slides out. Serve garnished with a sprig of mint and chocolate shavings.

CHOCOLATE-WAFER CRUSTS

MAKES ENOUGH FOR 6 SMALL TARTS

- 35 chocolate wafers (about 7½ ounces)
- 3 tablespoons sugar
- 4 tablespoons unsalted butter, melted

1. Preheat oven to 350°F. Process chocolate wafers in a food processor until fine crumbs form. Add sugar and butter, and process until combined.

2. Place six 2¾-by-2-inch ring molds on a rimmed baking sheet. Pat 5 to 6 tablespoons crumb mixture into each, pressing onto bottom and halfway up sides. Bake until crusts are fragrant, about 8 minutes. Transfer to a wire rack to cool completely before filling. Store at room temperature up to 1 day.

BEEF NEGIMAKI WITH ASPARAGUS

MAKES 2 DOZEN

- Coarse salt
- 24 thin stalks asparagus, or 12 thick stalks halved lengthwise
- ½ cup soy sauce
- ¼ cup sugar
- 1½ pounds beef tenderloin
- Freshly ground pepper
- 1 bunch scallions, green parts only, cut into 3½-inch lengths
- Daikon radish sprouts, for garnish (optional)

1. Bring a medium saucepan of water to a boil; add salt. Prepare an ice bath; set aside. Cut off asparagus ends to within 3½ inches from tips; discard ends. Add asparagus to boiling water; cook until bright green but still crisp, about 1 minute. Drain; transfer to ice bath to stop the cooking. Drain; set aside.

2. Make sauce: In a small bowl, whisk together soy sauce and sugar until sugar dissolves. Pour half the sauce into a dish; reserve for serving.

3. Cut tenderloin into ¼-inch-thick slices. Place one slice between two pieces of plastic wrap; pound meat lightly to an even thickness. Trim meat to a 2-by-4-inch rectangle. Repeat with remaining tenderloin.

4. Heat a grill or grill pan, or heat the broiler. Dip beef into sauce, and place on a clean work surface. Season with pepper. Arrange 1 scallion piece and 2 asparagus tips in opposite directions along one long end of beef so vegetables extend over edges; roll up into a log. Repeat process with remaining beef, sauce (save some for grilling), and vegetables.

5. Grill or broil negimaki, brushing with sauce and turning as needed, until beef is slightly charred, about 2 minutes for medium-rare. Garnish with radish sprouts; serve hot with reserved sauce on the side.

A PLENTIFUL BOWL

Long strands of vegetables accompany soba, or buckwheat noodles. The vegetables are prepared on a Japanese turning slicer or vegetable peeler, which create curly noodlelike strands; a vegetable peeler works well, too.

LONG-LIFE NOODLES

SERVES 6 TO 8

- 1 square (4 inches) dried kombu (dried seaweed), cleaned with a damp cloth
- 1 piece fresh ginger (4 ounces), thinly sliced, plus more peeled and grated for serving
- 2 small garlic cloves, thinly sliced
- 1 small bunch fresh cilantro (with roots)
- 2 cups dried bonito flakes
- 2 tablespoons prepared wasabi paste
- 1 pound soba noodles
- 2 tablespoons freshly squeezed lime juice
- Coarse salt
- 1 sweet potato (about 6 ounces), peeled and julienned
- 1 small daikon radish (about 7 ounces), peeled and julienned, plus daikon sprouts for garnish
- 2 cups baby tatsoi leaves or baby spinach leaves, stemmed
- 4 scallions, trimmed and thinly sliced
- Soy sauce

1. In a large saucepan over high heat, bring kombu, ginger, garlic, cilantro, and 10 cups water to a boil. Immediately remove kombu with tongs; discard. Add bonito flakes and wasabi, and stir. Reduce heat; simmer until broth is very flavorful, about 45 minutes. Strain broth through a fine sieve, discarding solids; return to saucepan. Set aside.

2. In large pot, bring 4 quarts water to a rolling boil over high heat. Add soba; gently stir with a wooden spoon to separate noodles. When water returns to a boil, reduce heat to medium; cook, stirring occasionally, until noodles are tender but firm, about 4 minutes. Drain noodles in a colander; rinse under cold water to stop the cooking.

3. Bring reserved broth to a simmer over medium heat. Add lime juice; season with salt. Add sweet potato and daikon; cook until softened, about 2 minutes. Add noodles; cook, stirring gently, until warmed through, about 1 minute. Add tatsoi; cook just until wilted, about 30 seconds. Transfer to a serving bowl; sprinkle with scallions. Serve with soy sauce, grated ginger, and daikon sprouts.

SESAME TOFU WITH MISO GLAZE

SERVES 8

In Japanese cooking, firm tofu is often pressed to extract excess water, condensing its flavor and texture. We use that technique here.

- 1 package firm tofu (14 ounces)
- 2 tablespoons white or red miso paste
- 1/4 cup plus 1/2 tablespoon vegetable oil
- 1/4 cup sesame seeds
- 1/4 cup rice-wine vinegar
- 2 tablespoons mirin
- 2 tablespoons tamari soy sauce
- 8 radishes, thinly sliced
- 4 scallions, pale-green and white parts only, halved lengthwise and cut into 1-inch julienne

1. Remove tofu from its package, discarding water, and place in a large colander lined with paper towels. Rest a small plate on top of tofu; weight with 3 pounds of cans. Let drain 1 hour at room temperature.

2. Remove tofu, and pat dry. Slice in half horizontally to create two equal pieces, and place on a baking sheet. In a small bowl, combine miso paste with ½ tablespoon oil until smooth. Use a small knife or offset spatula to smooth paste evenly over top of tofu. Press sesame seeds onto each piece, dividing evenly; set aside.

3. Make dressing: In a medium bowl, whisk together vinegar, mirin, soy sauce, and remaining ¼ cup oil. Set aside.

4. Heat broiler. Broil tofu just until seeds are golden brown, checking often. Remove; quarter each piece of tofu (for a total of eight pieces). Transfer tofu to serving plates, and garnish with radishes and scallions. Drizzle with dressing, and serve.

JAPANESE SALAD WITH WATERCRESS AND BAY SCALLOPS

SERVES 6 TO 8

If you have a skillet that's smaller than twelve inches, cook the scallops in smaller batches, using less oil in each so they will brown properly and won't steam.

- 1 piece fresh ginger (2½ inches), peeled
- 1½ tablespoons rice-wine vinegar
- 2½ tablespoons freshly squeezed lemon juice
- 1 teaspoon sugar
- 7 tablespoons vegetable oil
- 1 pound watercress (about 2 bunches), long stems removed, cut into 2-inch pieces
- 1 pound bay scallops
- Coarse salt and freshly ground pepper
- 6 ounces Japanese or seedless cucumber, thinly sliced crosswise

1. Make vinaigrette: Finely grate ginger into a medium bowl. Add vinegar, lemon juice, sugar, and 5 tablespoons oil; whisk to combine. Set aside. Separate watercress leaves, and transfer to a large bowl; set aside.

2. Heat a 12-inch skillet over medium-high heat; add 1 tablespoon oil. Season scallops with salt and pepper; cook half until golden on both sides, 4 to 6 minutes (if scallops release a large amount of liquid, pour it off and continue to cook). Remove scallops from skillet. Repeat with remaining tablespoon oil and scallops.

3. Drizzle watercress with vinaigrette. Add cucumber and scallops, and toss to combine. Serve immediately.

GREEN-TEA GRANITA

SERVES 6 TO 8

Look for matcha, or powdered green tea, in Asian markets or specialty food stores.

- 1½ cups sugar
- 2 teaspoons (about 5 grams) powdered green tea (matcha)
- ⅓ cup dry sake

1. Prepare an ice bath, and set aside. In a large saucepan, bring 6 cups water and the sugar to a boil over medium-high heat, stirring to dissolve sugar. Boil, stirring frequently, about 3 minutes. Pour hot sugar syrup into a large bowl, and whisk in powdered tea. Place bowl in the ice bath; let cool completely, stirring occasionally. Stir in sake, and pour mixture into a 9-by-13-inch metal pan or container. Cover with plastic wrap, and transfer to the freezer.

2. Freeze just until mixture begins to set, checking often, about 45 minutes. Use a fork to scrape the icy particles from sides of pan. Stir mixture well, and return to freezer. Continue scraping and stirring every 30 to 45 minutes until all liquid is frozen and texture is grainy, 3 to 3½ hours total.

GREEN-TEA SHORTBREAD LEAVES

MAKES 3 DOZEN

- 2 cups all-purpose flour, plus more for parchment paper
- 2 tablespoons powdered green tea (matcha)
- ½ teaspoon salt
- 1 cup (2 sticks) unsalted butter, room temperature
- ½ cup confectioners' or granulated sugar

1. Sift together flour, powdered tea, and salt into a small bowl; set aside. Place butter in the bowl of an electric mixer fitted with the paddle attachment; cream on medium speed until fluffy, 3 to 5 minutes. Add sugar; beat until very light and fluffy, scraping down sides of bowl with a spatula as needed, about 2 minutes. Add flour mixture; beat on low speed, scraping down sides of bowl as needed, until just incorporated and dough sticks together when squeezed with fingers.

2. Place a piece of parchment paper on a clean work surface; dust with flour. Roll out dough ¼ inch thick; chill in refrigerator or freezer until firm, about 30 minutes.

3. Preheat oven to 325°F. Line two baking sheets with parchment paper. Cut chilled dough with 2-inch leaf cutters. Using a wide spatula, transfer to baking sheets; chill until firm, about 15 minutes. Gather scraps together, reroll, chill, and cut more shapes.

4. Bake cookies until firm and barely starting to color, rotating baking sheets halfway through, 15 to 20 minutes. Let cool completely on a wire rack. Store cookies in an airtight container at room temperature up to 3 weeks.

TEMPLATES

CORNHUSK FLOWERS

Copy templates onto card stock at 100 percent. Cut out, and place template on slightly damp husk; cut out shapes. Using your fingers, cup and shape petals while they dry.

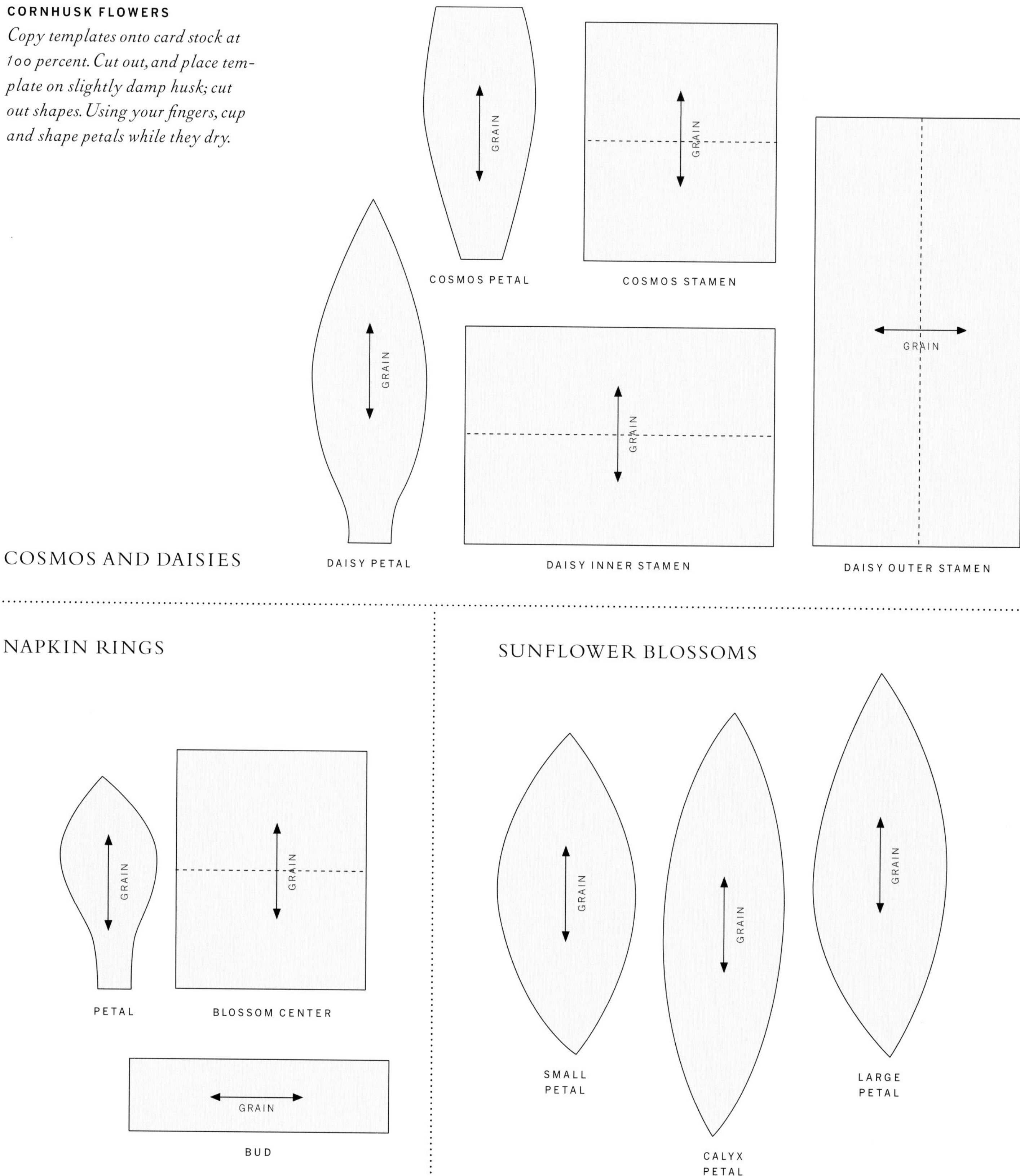

FAUX-GINGERBREAD ORNAMENTS

BIRD TEMPLATES *Photocopy these figures at 180 percent; trace onto card stock, and cut out. Punch holes for hanging. Place template over dough, and cut out shapes using a utility knife. Decorate with glitter and beads following our suggestions (unembellished areas are brown). The finished birds are pictured on page 82. To hang, knot a length of ribbon through hole, and tie to a tree branch.*

THE GUIDE

Items pictured but not listed may not be available or are from private collections. Addresses and telephone numbers of sources may change, as may availability of any item.

INTRODUCTION

PAGE 7

Burken glass SPAGHETTI JAR and Burken glass JARS, *from Ikea, 800-434-4532 or www.ikea-usa.com.* Martha Stewart Everyday STORAGE JARS, *from Kmart, 866-562-7848 or www.kmart.com.* GUM BALLS and King Leo PEPPERMINT STICKS, *from Dylan's Candy Bar, 1011 Third Avenue, New York, NY 10021, 646-735-0078 or www.dylanscandybar.com.* Old-Fashioned CANDY JARS (DNC007), and Clear Glass CAKE STANDS (KGP006), *from Martha Stewart: The Catalog for Living, 800-950-7130 or www.marthastewart.com.*

GOOD THINGS

PAGE 8

5/8" QUILLING PAPER (#356), *from Lake City Crafts, 417-725-8444 or www.quilling.com.* Similar QUILLING KIT (CQU001), *from Martha Stewart: The Catalog for Living, 800-950-7130 or www.marthastewart.com.*

PAGE 9

Martha Stewart Everyday striped WRAPPING PAPER, *from the Sugar Plum Dreams collection, from Kmart, 866-562-7848 or www.kmart.com.*

PAGE 10

Splendorette RIBBON ROLLS, 250 yd. each: 1 1/4" in emerald green (GG-BE-SR114EME); 3/4" in emerald green (GG-BE-SR34EME); 1 1/4" in hunter green (GG-BE-SR114HUN); and 3/4" in hunter green (GG-BE-SR34HUN), *from Superior Giftwrap, 866-443-8977 or www.superiorgiftwrap.com.*

A FAMILY GATHERS AT HOME FOR THE HOLIDAYS

Special thanks to Robert Fuller for the use of his vintage pickup truck.

PAGE 18

Red wax bag and white wax bag LUMINARIAS, *from RC Co., 800-356-7699 or www.luminarias.com.*

PAGE 19

DOILY CANDLE CUFFS (#514), by Mary Jane Collection, *from Artifacts; 800-678-4178 or www.artifactsinc.com. Easy-to-Make Decorative Paper Snowflakes* by Brenda Lee Reed (Dover; 1987), *from www.doverpublications.com.* RIBBONS, *from Masterstroke Canada, 866-249-7677 or www.masterstrokecanada.com.* CANDY CANES, *from Bobs Candies, 800-569-4033 or www.bobscandies.com.* STOCKINGS made from Carousel Stripe (#3954.01/5), *from Brunschwig & Fils, 800-538-1880 or www.brunschwig.com (to the trade only).* FLEECE ZIP PULLOVER (TA43893); FLEECE HAT (LC35343), *from L.L. Bean, 800-809-7057 or www.llbean.com.*

PAGE 20

Red Le Creuset FONDUE SET (#16926), *from Sur La Table, 800-243-0852 or www.surlatable.com.*

PAGE 21

19th-century FRENCH LIBRARY TABLE; yellow-painted FRENCH CHAIRS; and Swedish PRIMITIVE CHAIRS, *from Bountiful, 1335 Abbot Kinney Blvd., Venice, CA 90291, 310-450-3620 or www.bountifulhome.com.* "Elements" DINNER PLATES (#394246), and "Isabella" GOBLETS (#149993), *from Crate and Barrel, 800-967-6696 or www.crateandbarrel.com.* RUNNERS, made by Hamilton Dimity (#53021.01), *from Brunschwig & Fils, 800-538-1880 or www.brunschwig.com (to the trade only).*

PAGE 23

14-lb. HAM, *from HoneyBaked Ham, 800-343-4267.* Red SALAD BOWL (#135533), and SERVERS (#261248), *from Sur La Table, 800-243-0852 or www.surlatable.com.*

PAGE 25

BAKERS' TWINE, *from Wolf Paper and Twine, 212-675-4870.* BOXES, *from World Treasure Trading Company, 707-566-7888.*

TREE-TRIMMING DESSERT PARTY

PAGE 44

Star flower GOLD FOIL (DT16G), *from D. Blümchen and Company, P.O. Box 1210, Ridgewood, NJ 07451, 866-653-9627.*

A HOLIDAY BUFFET OF SOUTHWESTERN FAVORITES

PAGES 44-57

Garland's Oak Creek Lodge, 520-282-3343 or www.garlandslodge.com.

PAGE 45

PEPPERBERRIES *from Herbs, Spice, Everything Nice, 1142 Loraine Avenue, South Plainfield, NJ 07080, 908-753-5680.* De Árbol PEPPERS *from Kitchen/Market, 218 Eighth Avenue, New York, NY 10011, 888-468-4433 or www.kitchenmarket.com.* 19th-century CHINESE TABLE, *from Evergreen Antiques, 1249 Third Avenue, New York, NY 10021, 212-744-5664 or www.evergreenantiques.com.*

PAGE 46

MUGS, *from Global Table, 107 Sullivan Street, New York, NY 10012, 212-431-5839 or www.globaltable.com.*

PAGE 49

AMERICAN JELLY GLASS, *from L. Becker Flowers, 217 East 83rd Street, New York, NY 10028, 212-439-6001.*

PAGES 50-51

Glass BOWL; wooden PADDLES; and PLACE MATS, *from Pan American Phoenix, 857 Lexington Avenue, New York, NY 10021, 212-570-0300 or www.panamphoenix.com.* Aluminum TAMALERA (Mexican steamer) *from Kitchen/Market, 218 Eighth Avenue, New York, NY 10011, 888-468-4433 or www.kitchenmarket.com.* BAMBOO STEAMER, *from KamMan, 200 Canal Street, New York, NY 10013, 212-571-0330.*

PAGES 54-57

LARGE INDIAN CORN with husk; MINIATURE INDIAN CORN with and without husk; and OFF-WHITE and PURPLE HUSKS, *from Pipestem Creek, 7060 Highway 9, Carrington, ND 58421, 800-446-1986 or www.pipestemcreek.com ($10 minimum order).* 22-gauge white-cloth-wrapped STEM WIRE, 18" precut, and STEM TAPE in white and brown, *from Beverly's Crafts & Fabrics, 831-768-8439, 831-768-8428, or www.save-on-crafts.com.* 32-gauge clear sterling WIRE, *from Paramount Wire, 973-672-0500 or www.parawire.com.*

LATE-AFTERNOON LUNCH WITH FRIENDS

PAGE 60

Suomi white DINNER PLATES and SALAD PLATES, *by Rosenthal China, 800-804-8070 or www.rosenthalchina.com.*

AN OPEN HOUSE ON CHRISTMAS DAY

PAGE 71

Boys' vintage Burberry SWEATER, *from What Comes Around Goes Around, 212-343-9303 or www.wcaga.us.* Similar EUCALYPTUS WREATH WITH POMEGRANATES (XMG043), *from Martha Stewart: The Catalog for Living, 800-950-7130 or www.marthastewart.com.*

PAGE 72

Large Windsor GLASS BOWL (for punch), *from Simon Pearce, 877-452-7763 or www.simonpearce.com.*

PAGE 73

VINE-AND-BERRY SQUARE DISH, circa 1870, and SPODE PLATTERS with orange border, circa 1810, *from Bardith, 901 Madison Avenue, New York, NY 10021, 212-737-3775.* Round glass TEA-LIGHT HOLDERS (#1862054), and TEA LIGHTS (#1881611), *from Pier 1 Imports, 800-245-4595 or www.pier1.com.*

PAGE 74

VINE-AND-BERRY PLATE, circa 1870, and WEDGWOOD PLATE, circa 1810, *from Bardith, 901 Madison Avenue, New York, NY 10021, 212-737-3775.* Ivory Petassoun MATELASSE FABRIC (for tablecloth; #89462-008), *from Brunschwig & Fils, 800-538-1880 (to the trade only).*

PAGE 75

Danielle MATELESSE FABRIC, in Lemon (#46043-02), *from Brunschwig & Fils, 800-538-1880 (to the trade only).* Similar CRYSTAL GOBLETS (DTS090), *from Martha Stewart: The Catalog for Living, 800-950-7130 or www.marthastewart.com.*

PAGES 82-83

Premium GROUND CINNAMON, *from the Spice Barn, 866-670-9040 or www.spicebarn.com.* Similar GLASS GLITTER KIT (CGS001); similar HOLIDAY COOKIE DECORATIONS (KSS020); and Bulk GLASS GLITTER (CGS005), *from Martha Stewart: The Catalog for Living, 800-950-7130 or www.marthastewart.com.* Microfine Sparklerz GLITTER and MICROBEADS, *from Provo Craft/Creative Xpress, 800-563-8679.* Opaque deep-red SEED BEAD, *from the Bead Shop, 650-328-7925 or www.beadshop.com.* Plastic GLITTER in assorted colors, *from Dick Blick Art Materials, 800-828-4548 or www.dickblick.com.*

NEW YEAR'S EVE DINNER IN THE CITY

PAGES 84-95

Martha Stewart Everyday GLASS ORNAMENTS, 70 mm or 85 mm, *from Kmart, 866-562-7848 or www.kmart.com.* TRIPLE ICICLE DRIP (XXC002), *from Martha Stewart: The Catalog for Living, 800-950-7130 or www.marthastewart.com.* Santa ICE CRYSTALS (#4990542), *from Chase Products, 800-323-7136 or www.chaseproducts.com.* Crystal FROST SPRAY (#800), *from Design Master, P.O. Box 601, Boulder, CO 80306, 303-443-5214 for locations.*

PAGE 85

6'-by-9' heavy bouclé SISAL CARPET in Sage (#15010084), *from Restoration Hardware, 800-762-1005 or www.restorationhardware.com.* Duchamp 16" cube TABLES, by Rodolfo Dordoni for Minotti, *from See, 212-228-3600.* 56"-wide Somerset CHAIR FABRIC, in Puddle (#910038-10) and 51"-wide Lucia SOFA FABRIC in Pewter (#808002-06), *from Rogers & Goffigon, 203-532-8068 (to the trade only).* WINDOW SHADES and PILLOWS, *by Stefan Steil, stefansteil@yahoo.com.* MERCURY-GLASS LAMP and COMPOTE, *from Paterae, 458 Broome Street, New York, NY 10013, 212-941-0880.*

PAGE 86

ANTIQUE MIRROR, *from Bucks County Antique Center, Route 202, Lahaska, PA 18931, 215-794-9180.* Blown-glass VASES, *from Evergreen Antiques, 1249 Third Avenue, New York, NY 10021, 212-744-5664 or www.evergreenantiques.com.*

PAGE 87

Hanging PHOTOGRAPHS, *by Victor Schrager, 212-925-3028 or www.victorschrager.com.* FRAMES, *by Bark Frameworks, 270 Lafayette Street, Suite 500, New York, NY 10012, 212-431-9080 or www.barkframeworks.com (by appointment only).* Fresh FLYING-FISH ROE with wasabi, and Russian GOLDEN PIKE ROE, *from Russ & Daughters, 800-787-7229 or www.russanddaughters.com.* 19th-century Swedish painted drop-front WOODEN DESK, *from L. Becker Flowers, 217 East 83rd Street, New York, NY 10028, 212-439-6001.*

PAGE 88

Glass VOTIVES, *from L. Becker Flowers, 217 East 83rd Street, New York, NY 10028; 212-439-6001.*

PAGE 89

Palma CHAIR with LEATHER SEAT by Modénature (#4563), *from Intérieurs, 212-343-0800 or www.interieurs.com.* Leiso Austria woven texture SEAT-CUSHION FABRIC (#83231-924), in Gris, *by Gaston y Daniela, from Brunschwig & Fils, 800-538-1880 or www.brunschwig.com (to the trade only).* Blue French soft paste PORCELAIN BOWLS, *from Sentimento, 306 East 61st Street, New York, NY 10021, 212-750-3111 (to the trade only).* Wedgwood QUEEN'S WARE, 5-piece place setting (KWE001), and 20-piece place setting (KWE015), *from Martha Stewart: The Catalog for Living, 800-950-7130 or www.marthastewart.com.*

PAGE 93

ORCHIDS, *from L. Becker Flowers, 217 East 83rd Street, New York, NY 10028; 212-439-6001.*

PAGE 95

12" square double-flat 12-gauge WIRE WREATH FORM (#60RIQ12), *from Oregon Wire Products, 800-458-8344 or www.oregonwireproducts.com.* Perfect Touch SILVER SPRAY (#1537), and En Vogue metallic floral SPRAY PAINT in Antique Gold (#1562), *by Floralife, from B&J Florist Supply, 103 West 28th Street, New York, NY 10001, 212-564-6086.*

A JAPANESE LUNCH WITH GOOD WISHES FOR THE NEW YEAR

PAGE 97

CHOPSTICK RESTS, *from Broadway Panhandler, 477 Broome Street, New York, NY 10013, 866-266-5927.* SILVER CHOPSTICKS, *from Tiffany & Co., 727 Fifth Avenue, New York, NY 10022, 800-843-3269.* SILVER and WOOD CHOPSTICKS, *from Barneys New York, 660 Madison Avenue, New York, NY 10021, 212-826-8900.* UPHOLSTERY, *by D&F Workroom, 150 West 25th Street, 2nd floor, New York, NY 10001, 212-352-0160.* CUSHION FOAM, *from Economy Foam and Futons Center, 173 East Houston Street, New York, NY 10002, 212-473-4462.*

PAGES 98-99

ORIGAMI PAPER, *from Hanko Designs, 510-523-5603 or www.hankodesigns.com,* or from *Aitoh Company (wholesale only),* or *available nationwide at Hobby Lobby, A.C. Moore, and Michael's.* SILK CORDING, *from M&J Trimming, 1008 Sixth Avenue, New York, NY 10018, 800-965-8746 or www.mjtrim.com.* LACE RICE PAPER, *from Kate's Paperie, 888-941-9169 or www.katespaperie .com for locations.*

PAGE 101

BLACK BOWL *by Keiko Hasegawa, from Egg, 36 Kinnerton Street, London, England SWIX 8ES, 011-44-171-235-9315.*

PAGE 105

JAPANESE TABLE, *from Palisander Ltd., 979 Third Avenue, New York, NY 10022, 212-755-0120.* DISHES, *from Takashimaya New York, 693 Fifth Avenue, New York, NY 10022, 800-753-2038.* Woven BAMBOO MAT, *from Sinotique, 19 Mott Street, New York, NY 10013, 212-587-2393.*

RECIPES

PAGES 108-135

SILPAT BAKING MAT (KSP002), *from Martha Stewart: The Catalog for Living, 800-950-7130 or www.marthastewart.com.* DRIED MASA HARINA for tamales; DRIED CORNHUSKS; DRIED AVOCADO LEAVES; DRIED CHIPOLTE CHILES; CANNED CHIPOLTE CHILES; and IBARRA CHOCOLATE, *from Kitchen/Market, 888-468-4433 or www.kitchenmarket.com.* VENISON, *from D'Artagnan, 800-327-8246.* 10" BAMBOO STEAMER, *from Katagiri; 224 East 59th Street, New York, NY 10022, 212-838-5453 or www .katagiri.com.* 2" star COOKIE CUTTER (#607834), and SANDING SUGAR (#49549), *from Sweet Celebrations, 800-328-6722 or www.sweetc.com.* LEAF STENCIL (AT-1390), *from Candyland Crafts, 908-685-0410 or www.candylandcrafts.com.* Standard GRAINING ROCKER (SY31740), *from O-Gee Paint, 866-666-1935.* ACETATE, *from Pearl Paint, 308 Canal Street, New York, NY 10013, 212-431-7932.* Smoked RAINBOW TROUT, *from Petrossian Paris, 212-245-2217 or www .petrossian.com.* 10" fluted TART DISH (CBQM-10), and 4"-by-14" TART PAN with removable bottom (ABTF-T-14R), *from Bridge Kitchenware, 214 East 52nd Street, New York, NY 10022, 800-274-3435 or www.bridgekitchenware.com.* Smoked HAM, *from Harrington's of Vermont, 802-434-4444 or www.harringtonham.com.* 9 1/2"-by-13" rimmed QUARTER-SHEET PAN (#558550), and 12"-by-17" rimmed HALF-SHEET PAN (#558551), *from Broadway Panhandler, 477 Broome Street, New York, NY 10013, 866-266-5927 or www.broadwaypanhandler.com.* TURBINADO SUGAR, *from Whole Foods Market, 250 7th Avenue, New York, NY 10001, 212-924-5969 or www.wholefoodsmarket.com.* Metal RING MOLDS (S-272), 2 3/4"-by-2," *from Kerekes Bakery & Restaurant Equipment, 6103 15th Avenue, Brooklyn, NY 11219, 800-525-5556 or www.kerekesequip .com.* JAPANESE TURNING SLICER or SHAVER, *from Katagiri, 224 East 59th Street, New York, NY 10022, 212-838-5453.* WASABI; DAIKON; DRIED BONITO FLAKES; DRIED KOMBU; and SOBA NOODLES; *from Uwajimaya, 800-889-1928 or www.uwajimaya.com.* GREEN TEA MATCHA, *from Takashimaya New York, 693 Fifth Avenue, New York, NY 10022, 800-753-2038.*

INDEX

Note: Page references in *italics* are photographs.

CONTRIBUTORS

Executive Creative Director: Eric A. Pike
Editor: Ellen Morrissey
Art Directors: Mary Jane Callister and Linda Kocur
Writer: Alice Gordon
Associate Editor: Christine Moller
Associate Art Director: Amber Blakesley
Copy Editor: Robert Bowe
Senior Design Production Associate: Duane Stapp

Thank you to all who generously lent their time, talent, and energy to the creation of this book, among them Jennifer Aaronson, Roger Astudillo, Evelyn Battaglia, Tara Bench, Stephana Bottom, Randi Brookman, Elizabeth Brownfield, Dora Braschi Cardinale, Shawn Chavez, Denise Clappi, Peter Colen, James Dunlinson, John Dunn, Natalie Ermann, Richard P. Fontaine, Melañio Gomez, Tanya Graff, Angela Gubler, Eric Hutton, Jennifer J. Jarett, Megen Lee, Charlyne Mattox, Marcie McGoldrick, Jim McKeever, Hannah Milman, Pamela Morris, Elizabeth Parson, Ayesha Patel, Meg Peterson, George D. Planding, Jamie Prokell, Debra Puchalla, Madhu Puri, Meera Rao, Brooke H. Reynolds, Ben Rice, Lynn Ringland, Margaret Roach, Scot Schy, Lauren Shields, Colleen Shire, Lauren Podlach Stanich, Stefan Steil, Harley Swedler, Susan Sugarman, Susie Theodorou, Gael Towey, Alison Vanek, Sarina Vetterli, Michelle Wong, and Sheila Yun. Thanks also to Oxmoor House, Satellite Graphics, AGT.seven, and R.R. Donnelley. And thank you, Martha, for teaching us what matters most when it comes to celebrating the holidays.

PHOTOGRAPHY

ANTONIS ACHILLEOS: page 82 (left)

SANG AN: pages 65, 125

CHRISTOPHER BAKER: pages 5 (top and bottom left), 32, 33, 35 (top and bottom left), 40–42, 43 (left two), 45, 47 (center), 48, 49, 54–57, 96, 99 (bottom left), 104, 105, 107 (top left)

EARL CARTER: front and back covers, pages 4, 7, 10, 11 (bottom two), 12, 13, 14 (top two), 15, 16–26, 27 (bottom right), 29 (bottom right)

CARLTON DAVIS: page 131

DANA GALLAGHER: pages 8, 9, 11 (top), 14 (bottom), 50, 51, 108

GENTL & HYERS: pages 97, 101, 134

LISA HUBBARD: page 36 (top left)

THIBAULT JEANSON: pages 2, 84, 85, 87 (all but bottom left), 88 (all but top left), 89, 93–95

RICHARD GERHARD JUNG: page 144

KEN KOCHEY: pages 44, 46, 47 (all but center)

JOSH TITUS: pages 80 (top left two), 82 (right), 83

ANNA WILLIAMS: pages 3, 5 (top and bottom right), 6, 27 (all but bottom right), 28, 29 (all but bottom right), 30, 31, 34, 35 (right), 36 (bottom left), 37, 38, 39, 43 (right three), 52, 53, 58–64, 66–79, 80 (all but top left two), 81, 86, 87 (bottom left), 88 (top left), 90–92, 98, 99 (all but bottom left), 100, 102, 103, 107 (all but top left), 122, 132, 138, 141